MW01165893

The Pursuit of a Christian

Witness Lee

Living Stream Ministry
Anaheim, CA

First Edition, May 2001.

ISBN 0-7363-1277-3

Published by

Living Stream Ministry
2431 W. La Palma Ave., Anaheim, CA 92801 U.S.A.
P. O. Box 2121, Anaheim, CA 92814 U.S.A.

Printed in the United States of America

01 02 03 04 05 06 07 / 10 9 8 7 6 5 4 3 2 1

CONTENTS

PREFACE

This book is a translation of messages given in Chinese by Brother Witness Lee in the summer of 1950 in Taipei, Taiwan. These messages were not reviewed by the speaker.

CHAPTER ONE

THE PURSUIT OF A CHRISTIAN

THE GOAL OF A CHRISTIAN
DETERMINING THE MODEL OF A CHRISTIAN

It is of great importance for Christians to know their inclination. What is the inclination of man's heart? What is man seeking after? What is his lifelong goal? These are great questions of human life and the so-called philosophy of life. What should man really take as his purpose? Throughout the history of mankind, there have been varied opinions about this, but until now there is still no definitive answer. Even though successful and famous people have their own individual goals, they are unable to offer us an accurate answer as to what really is the goal of human life.

Christians have God living within them; they have God's life in them. Hence, they may be considered the remarkable and exceptional ones among men. With these ones, what is the goal of their human life? They read the Bible and pray daily, and they also meet together and offer petitions regularly. What actually is their inclination? What do they want to obtain in their pursuit? I am afraid even they are not able to give us a clear answer. Some may say that they believed in Jesus to find someone to whom they can entrust themselves. This is because they are convinced that those who do not believe in Jesus do not have God and that those who do not have God have no one to whom they can commit themselves. Others may say that they became Christians in order to obtain peace and enjoy blessings. They consider that those who are without God have neither peace nor blessings; those who have God, however, will obtain peace and enjoy the God-given blessings if they pray to God whenever they face some difficulties. It seems that to be a Christian is just to hope for these things.

What is God's intention for His children? What does He want His children to focus on and seek after? In other words, what does God want us Christians to obtain in our pursuit? If Christians fail to ascertain this goal, then it is difficult for them to be normal, genuine Christians. This is because if a Christian does not have a proper goal, his direction and his way will be wrong; consequently, he will not conduct himself as a Christian. Therefore, in addition to church history, Christians should know the proper Christian goal so that they may establish the proper Christian model. After all, the model of a Christian is determined by his goal.

MAN BEING CREATED EXCLUSIVELY FOR GOD

There is a great problem, however, that hinders man from knowing this goal. For instance, if someone tosses a small diamond or pearl into a pile of rice grains, it will be difficult for us to find the gem. However, if he puts the diamond or pearl in his hand, then the gem can be clearly seen. The Christian goal is truly a mystery in the universe because it has been hidden in a countless number of matters and things. Consequently, many lose sight of the goal because their eyes have become blurred. Although there is a great distinction between the goal and the myriad of things, it is difficult to identify the goal because it has been mixed in with so many things. If we know the Bible, however, we can see that man was created exclusively for God. For example, a microphone is used exclusively for speaking or singing. In the universe man was created with a unique purpose. The microphone may be altered to be used for other functions but man cannot be changed for other purposes. Once the purpose of man is changed, the original purpose of God's creation of man is nullified.

In Genesis we are clearly told that man was created for God. Therefore, man's goal is God; man must pursue God and long for God. If man receives God, he will have the inner satisfaction, joy, and peace, his eyes will be enlightened, and all his problems will be resolved. Please remember that before the fall of man and his subsequent removal from God's presence, man was in fellowship with God. At that time man was filled with satisfaction and joy. However, because man fell away from God, there was a distance between man and God. Thus, man was alienated from God. Thereafter, man lost his satisfaction, joy, and enjoyment of God.

We can find out how music came about if we study the Bible carefully. Music came into existence after man had lost the enjoyment of God due to his fall and removal from God's presence. Man invented music for self-amusement because he had been alienated from God and had lost his joy in God. Thus, music was brought in because man had lost God (Gen. 4:21). A person who has God has music. The Bible tells us that the best music is God Himself. A person who has God can make melody in his heart. Millions of saved ones can testify that they sing and make melody because they have God as their music. If a person does not have God, he does not have music; he can neither sing nor play music. Therefore, he has to seek after music outside of God. The reason that man seeks after music is that he does not have God. He seeks after amusement because he has lost God.

There is a Chinese idiom which literally means "drinking poisonous wine to quench one's thirst." It is used to describe a person who acts against principle for a moment's relief or comfort and thus brings endless sufferings upon himself. Having lost God, man has an unquenchable thirst in his inner being. What can he do then? The only alternative he has is to "drink poisonous wine." I believe that even today there are so many friends around us who attend theaters, go to dances, or play mah-jongg. Their participation in all these forms of amusement proves that they have lost God and that there is a great distance between them and God. Whenever we ask others to provide us a little pleasure or sympathy, this proves that we do not have God—we have lost God. No one would look for more water immediately after he has drunk to the full. If we are still looking for water, this proves that we have not drunk to the full and that we are still thirsty. The fact that people are seeking all kinds of amusements proves that they do not have God. I have seen some people who find pleasure in riches. These kind of people do not like dancing, going to bars, or playing mah-jongg; they only enjoy seeing a lot of money in front of them. When they count their money and examine their bank deposits, they become exhilarated. Others find pleasure in music; as long as they have music, they can forget about everything else. Still others focus their interest on literature. Therefore, we may say that everyone who has left God is always occupied by certain hobbies. There is no exception to this. Regardless of whether they are men or women, young or old, highly educated or barely educated, no one is without a hobby; everyone has something that he loves. A certain old man may care for nothing but a string of pearls. It does not matter if the weather is hot or cold, he likes to hold the pearls just the same. It seems that without the pearls he is at a loss to know what to do. Why is this? This is because man's heart cannot be empty. This is true even with an old man. Although he no longer desires anything in his heart, his heart remains empty and needs to be occupied and filled with something.

MAN'S HEART INCLINING TO GOD

Man's heart ought to be occupied and filled with God. If a person allows God to occupy his heart, other things will not come in. Let me use an illustration: While I am staying in my room, if a cat comes, I will chase it away. If a dog comes, I will also chase it away. If a pig comes, I will drive it away all the more. If I do not stay in my room, however, then the cat, the dog, and even the pig will come in. Therefore, man's heart ought to be occupied by God; otherwise, many things will come in. If we examine the hearts of men, we will find out that no human heart is empty. For this very reason, man becomes confused, his vision is blurred, and he is unable to discern his own inclination.

In reality man's heart is like the sticky paper set out to catch flies in summer. Everything that comes into contact with the flypaper gets stuck. Whether it is a strand of hair, a feather, or a handkerchief, whenever it comes into contact with the flypaper, it gets stuck. It is the same with man's heart. When man's heart touches literature, literature is stuck to it. When man's heart touches money, money is stuck to it. Man's heart is bewildered because so many different things are stuck to it. For example, a wife's heart is filled with her husband, children, house, money, clothes, refrigerator, and car. In addition, she wants the Lord. Thus, how can the eyes of her heart not be blurred? It is really difficult for man's heart to be empty. When a person is young, his heart is wild; when he becomes old, his heart is blurred.

Once when Charles Spurgeon was preaching, he said, "Look at this man here! His feet are grown in his heart!" Everyone stood up to look but did not see anything unusual. Then he explained, "Man's feet are for walking on the earth and man's heart ought not to touch the earth, yet today all the things of the earth have come into man's heart. This is why I say that man's feet are grown in man's heart." Is this a joke? I often ask a child, "Do you want the Lord Jesus?" He replies, "Yes, I want the Lord Jesus." Then I ask again, "Do you want some clothes?" He says, "Yes, I want some clothes." Again, I ask, "Do you want some dollar bills?" He answers, "Yes, I want some dollar bills." Is this not a case of "the feet growing in the heart"? All our hearts are impure. This impurity does not necessarily mean that we have sins and filthiness. Perhaps we do not have any sin or filthy thing, but we have many interests and pursuits. In Genesis, after man had lost God due to the fall, he began to seek many other things as replacements. As a result, several thousand years of human history show us that after leaving God, man fell into the materialistic world and has not been able to rescue himself.

MAN FALLING INTO MATERIAL THINGS
AND INTO SINS

Man's fall resulted in two situations: one is that man fell into material things, and the other is that he fell into sins. Material things are for man's enjoyment. If man has God, he does not need material enjoyment. Since man has lost God and is without God, he needs material enjoyment. Material things as replacements of God are counterfeits. Those who stress material enjoyment seek satisfaction and solace in the material world because they do not have God. A person who has God puts the material things aside. When man's flesh craves worldly enjoyment, it leads to lusts. Someone asked me if it is all right to go to a play. I said it is not. Then he said that going to a play is not sinful. It is true that the play itself may not be sinful, but it can arouse your lust and lead you to sin. Many people like to go to movies, some of which are not necessarily sinful. However, after going several times, their lust will be aroused. In the same way, putting on beautiful clothes and using cosmetics are not necessarily sinful. Such enjoyment, however, can arouse the lusts and result in sin. The enjoyment of material things always leads to sin. This is an unalterable principle.

The most licentious people are those who have the highest enjoyment in material things. They stress the enjoyment in food, clothing, housing, and transportation, and eventually they are overtaken by their lusts. Therefore, the result of man's fall into material things is that man falls into sins. Material things develop man's lusts. All kinds of material things have been organized, systematized, and constituted into a material world. Man exists in the world solely for his living, which is maintained by food, clothing, shelter, and transportation. When man has a problem in his living, he has a problem in his enjoyment. If he does not have enough to eat, cannot keep himself warm, has no place to live, and has no means for traveling, this means that the matters of food, clothing, housing, and transportation are still unresolved. These are matters relating to material enjoyment.

Material enjoyment has developed into a system which the Bible calls the *cosmos,* meaning the "world." All kinds of material things have become a system to ensnare man. This is the world. The world incites man's lusts. When man's lusts are incited, it is easy for man to fall into sin. When man's lusts appear, there is no way for man to escape sin. Therefore, applying cosmetics or going to a play is not sin, but after doing these things a few more times, sin enters. Man's falling into sin consists of two aspects: one aspect is enjoyment and the other aspect is sin. Some manifest their lusts in a crude way, without any "cosmetics" or "adornment," while others manifest their lusts in a "refined" and "noble" way. In either case they are all in an enjoyment which brings in lusts and results in sin. In conclusion, wherever there is the enjoyment of material things, there is lust and there is also sin.

THE CHRISTIAN GOAL BEING GOD HIMSELF

The problem today is that material enjoyment indeed brings in the lusts of the world. Moreover, man has fallen into the world of material things. A shortage of food and lack of clothing, however, are real personal problems. Under these circumstances, how should Christians live on earth? Some describe the heart of the Chinese people as a heart focused on money. They say that the Chinese and the Jews are the only two peoples on this earth who really love money and that the Chinese, in particular, worship gods in order to get rich. Now I am afraid that some have believed in Jesus in order to acquire wealth; the testimonies of these ones are not edifying at all. For example, someone said, "Yesterday morning I purchased a load of textiles, but by the afternoon the price went up. Thank the Lord that I have made a lot of money." Take another example: An elderly woman prays for her son who is out of town for business, "O God, may You keep him safe, prevent him from any accidents, and bless his business. You know our family of ten all depend upon him for our living." Actually, this kind of testimony and prayer is not according to God's desire. If God is merciful to you, He will not make you rich, because wealth is Satan in disguise. To put it bluntly, that is the world and that is sin; that is not really a blessing. Because our hearts are not pure, we always expect God to bless us and give us peace. Those who worship Buddha chant and beg, hoping that the gods who bestow blessings and peace will respond to all their pleas. Christians, however, must not pray like that because that kind of prayer is not pleasing to God. The Bible says, "For what shall a man be profited if he gains the whole world, but forfeits his soul-life?" (Matt. 16:26). If a person wants to follow the Lord, he must sell all his possessions and give to the poor, and then he will have treasure in the heavens (19:21).

Christians today are so pitiful that they actually esteem that which the early saints cast away. In Ecclesiastes chapter

one Solomon declared that all things under the sun are a
vanity of vanities (v. 2). If God were to give the material
things to us, He would be giving us vanity. In the New Testament, Paul, a man who knew God, said that material things
are refuse, dung, and stinky, worthless things (Phil. 3:7-8).
Many Christians today, however, consider these stinky
things treasures. This is because man, having fallen into the
enjoyment of material things, cannot discern the true nature
of these things. Therefore, some are even bewildered and ask,
"Do you really mean to say that we should not care about our
food and about our living? Why should we embrace a religion
if it cannot take care of our living?" Many people have asked
the same questions. This only indicates the pitiful situation
of men who have fallen into the snare of material things.
God's salvation is to deliver us from the fallen condition of the
material world, just as He has delivered us from our lusts.
Therefore, Christians should take nothing else but God Himself as their goal.

THE CHRISTIAN MODEL

Such model Christians appeared in the first two to three
centuries. They did not care for anything other than Christ;
they gave up their wealth and fame and were willing to suffer
hunger and martyrdom. By the thirteenth and fourteenth
centuries, there was still this kind of Christian. One example
is Francis of Assisi. He was from a wealthy family and had
received a great inheritance from his father. One day in his
meditation a revelation came to him. He saw that a person
will lose God if he gains wealth and will have no room for
wealth if he gains God. Francis had found the goal of human
life, which is just God Himself. He realized that if he wanted
anything outside of God, he would lose God. That day the
Lord told him, "Sell all your possessions." In a determined
manner he responded, "Lord, I will sell all my possessions to
follow You."

Another time, when Francis was meditating before God,
someone teased him, saying that he was thinking about getting married. He answered, "You are right! I was thinking
about being engaged to a girl whose name is Poverty. In fact, I

have just been engaged to Poverty." After saying this, he got up and on that very day gave all his possessions away to the poor. Many Christians were touched by him and responded in the same way. This is the Christian model and goal. If God's children want to gain God, they must forsake their material wealth and willingly become poor. Air cannot get into a cup which is filled with water; the water must be poured out before air can get into the cup. May God have mercy upon us so that we can see this reality.

Since we are children of God, our goal is neither enjoyment nor peace but God Himself. Perhaps some will say that they cannot believe in this kind of Christianity. And yet still so many have believed in Christ. In the last two thousand years tens of thousands of Christians have willingly become poor to follow the Lord. Today if we desire to take the way of recovery, we must also have this kind of vision and burden and be able to testify, saying, "All things are refuse! What my heart pursues is neither peace nor blessings but God Himself." John Bunyan was a well-known figure in English literary history and the author of *The Pilgrim's Progress*. It is believed that on one occasion he cried out loudly, "O Heaven, come! O Earth, come! I will praise the Lord whom I serve if He leads me to heaven; I will still praise Him even if He puts me in hell." He cared neither for heaven nor for hell; he cared only for God. He wanted neither the enjoyment in the present age nor the blessings in the coming age but only God Himself. This is the model of the Christians, and this is also the pursuit of the Christians.

CHAPTER TWO

FOUR THINGS
THAT A CHRISTIAN POSSESSES

After a Christian has been saved, he should at least have some knowledge concerning several fundamental matters: first, Christ; second, the Bible; third, the church; and fourth, Christians. Besides knowing Christ, the Bible, and the church, a good Christian should also have a clear understanding of what a Christian is, how to be a Christian, and what kind of living a Christian should have. Therefore, we may say that Christ, the Bible, the church, and fellow Christians are four things in a Christian's possession. All these four items are indispensable.

A Christian possesses these things not just in his mind; rather, he has these four things because he has the Lord Jesus living in him. Many are not clear about this point and thus do not know what a Christian is. A Christian is man plus God. Christians have not only the human element; their element is man plus Christ. Only those who have God added into them are called Christians. The fundamental difference between Christians and non-Christians lies only in the elements within them. A non-Christian is merely human; he is purely a human being. A Christian, however, is not just a human but has Christ, the incarnated One, within him.

We all know that the church as the Body of Christ is the enlargement of the principle of Christ and that Christians are the constituents of the church. Every Christian is a member of the Body, and the Body is the sum total of all the members. Thus, in terms of the Body, its element is the enlargement of Christ; in terms of the members, their element is also Christ. The element of the church is the enlargement of the principle of Christ. The principle of Christ is God being added into man. Therefore, Christians are those who have Christ within them. If a person calls himself a Christian yet does not have Christ as an element in him, then he is a Christian in name but not in reality.

A CHRISTIAN BEING A PERSON
WHO HAS CHRIST WITHIN

A Christian is one who has Christ in him. The Greek word for *Christian* is *Christianos,* a word formed from Latin. The ending *ianos,* denoting an adherent of someone, was applied to slaves belonging to the great families in the Roman Empire. Later, some began to call the followers of Christ *Christianoi* (Christians), adherents of Christ. Strictly speaking, Christians are simply "Christ-men"—those who belong to Christ.

Most people think that to be a Christian is to be a disciple of Christ, just as to be a Confucianist is to be a disciple of Confucius and to be a Socratic is to be a disciple of Socrates. Actually, being a disciple of Confucius or Socrates is different from being a disciple of Christ Jesus. All those who desire to follow Christ and be His disciples must have Christ. Only those who have Christ can be disciples of Christ. If we do not have the life of Christ, there is no way to learn Christ. If we have His life, then we can be His disciples and learn from Him. Disciples of Christ are those who have Christ within them as their life, their power, their preferences, and their everything. Such people are the expression of Christ.

Therefore, a Christian is one who contains Christ. If a cup does not contain tea, we cannot call it a teacup, and it would be deceiving to call it as such. A Christian is a Christ-man, a man with Christ. During the war, I met a French brother who could speak a little Mandarin. On the day we met, the person who introduced us said to me, "This is a French brother." The brother from France replied immediately, "I am not a Frenchman but a heavenly-kingdom-man." Of course, a saved person is a person of the heavenly kingdom. However, this is merely an objective knowledge. We must know that we are just like teacups and we have Christ as the tea in us. When others see us, we are just "cups" outwardly, without any flavor, yet after a few sips of us, they have drunk of Christ as the "tea." Anyone who does not have Christ is not a Christ-man. If someone claims that he is a Christ-man yet does not have Christ in him, then he is the greatest deceiver in the world. This is just like a person who is penniless yet exclaims, "I am a wealthy man! I am very rich!" Today, the same thing also happens in Christianity. Many do not have Christ in them yet claim they are Christians. Then how should a person who has Christ within conduct himself, and how should he live? The answer is very simple. In all things he should inquire of the Lord and have fellowship with Him. In particular, the new believers should have such a practice. In your daily contact with others, whether with your spouse or the brothers and sisters in the church, you should often ask, "Lord, are You happy with what I am going to do? Are You pleased with what I am about to say?" These words are simple yet precious.

Since we have been saved and have become Christ-men, we should ask ourselves often in our daily living, "When I say this word, does it please the Christ who is within me? When I do this thing, does it make Christ, who is in me, happy?" Before two people are married, they are independent of each other. Each one can decide according to his or her preference when to wake up, when to go to bed, what to eat, and when to come home. They are free from each other's control. Once they are married, however, they have to take care of each other's feeling. The wife has to consider whether her husband will be unhappy about her coming home so late and about the clothes she wears; likewise, the husband has to take his wife into consideration in the same matters. If the marital relationship is such, how much more should our walk and living be, since the Lord has entered into us and become united with us.

A CHRISTIAN HAVING CHRIST

First, a person who is a Christian must have Christ. After having Christ, we must always inquire of the Lord, seeking His approval in whatever we do in our daily living. This is because when we have Christ, we represent Him in everything we do. His pleasure and approval are absolutely important and necessary. Please remember that the Lord within us is our great protection and immense wisdom. Real Christians can all testify that many times while they are inquiring of the Lord, they have the inner wisdom, inner enlightenment, and inner presence of the Lord. Many foolish people do foolish things because they neglect the Lord who lives in them and care only for their own preferences and desires. A person is foolish if he acts independently of the Lord and apart from the Lord. A person will obtain wisdom, however, if he is willing to put himself aside and ask the Lord, "Do You want me to do this? Will You be happy if I do not do it?"

In the present crooked generation and during this time when the situation of the church is so dark, a person who desires to properly serve God finds it truly difficult to make a decision whenever he encounters a problem. It seems that almost every day he finds himself at a crossroads or in a dilemma. His only salvation is to pray unceasingly and ask, "Lord, which way do You prefer? Lord, is this what pleases You?" I can testify that sometimes for the whole night, even though I was lying in bed, my heart was before the Lord. In order to deal with a troublesome situation I was before the Lord all night, asking, "Lord, will You be pleased with this decision? Will You be pleased with a different decision?" Many times the Lord would say, "I am not pleased," but at other times He would say, "I am pleased."

Many people find it difficult to believe that God exists, but for us it is even more difficult to believe otherwise. These past few days, a brother who is a bricklayer has been repairing my house. One day I asked him, "You have been working like this every day. Is this what you want?" He sighed and said, "I work because I am poor. How blessed it would be if I were rich." I told him, "You really do not know Christ. Money is not necessarily a blessing. Being wealthy does not necessarily mean being blessed. We are Christians. Only those who have Christ are blessed." Unfortunately, many people are indeed Christians and have Christ within them, but because they do not have enough of Him, they are just like those who are without Christ. They do not bring any of their problems to the

Lord. It is as if there is no difference whether or not they have the Lord.

There was a couple who had just been married, and the husband began to complain about his wife to others, saying, "There is no one like her. She goes wherever she wants and does whatever she desires. She does not care a bit about me." Many Christians are like this. There is hardly any difference between having Christ and not having Christ. They do whatever they like, completely ignoring Christ's existence. Although they have Christ in them, they disregard Him. They say things as they like, they play politics as they desire, and they treat others as they wish; they do not care a bit how Christ feels. The only difference between them and the unbelievers is that the unbelievers behave recklessly in a manifest way, while they as Christians care for their faces and thus behave recklessly in a hidden way. However, please remember that we who have Christ should take Christ instead of morality as our standard, because the standard of Christ is higher than that of morality. Many times what morality allows, Christ disallows. Therefore, I hope that we will all learn to inquire of the Lord. Even in choosing what clothes to wear, we should learn to ask the Lord. This is the reality of allowing Christ to reign in us.

A CHRISTIAN HAVING THE BIBLE

Second, a Christian surely has the Bible. Unfortunately, many have the Bible in their hands or on their bookshelves but not in their heart. Some have been saved for many years, but they have read only up to Genesis chapter twenty in the Old Testament and up to Matthew chapter two in the New Testament. One day I told some Christians that Matthew chapter twenty-eight says that the Lord Jesus was resurrected and chapter twenty-nine says that He ascended to the heavens, and they all nodded their heads. So I said, "Alas! Your Bible is different from mine. Yours has twenty-nine chapters while mine has only twenty-eight." Then they stared at me dumbfounded. This proves that many Christians do not have the Bible within them because they do not read the Bible.

Besides Christ, Christians must have the Bible, and they must read it diligently. God has shown us mercy by giving us not only His only begotten Son but also the Bible. Thus, in addition to Christ, we have the Bible. In the universe besides our dear Lord, nothing else is more precious than the Bible. All who are Christ-men should always meditate on the words of the Bible so that they may be wise unto salvation, be preserved, and be protected. I hope that everyone who treasures the Lord's words will spend time reading the Bible and will learn to check everything with the Bible to see what it says.

A certain co-worker was greatly used by God because when he was young he consecrated himself to God to do everything absolutely according to the Bible. He said, "From now on I do not belong to the world, nor do I belong to any man. I just want to please God; I will not do anything that does not please Him." In the Bible he read something about what we should wear but could not find anything about wearing hats. As a result, regardless of how cold the weather was, he would not wear a hat. This may sound like a joke; the principle, though, is correct. However, do not misunderstand and think that I am saying that you should not wear hats. What the brother did was an indication of his absolute respect for the Bible.

The principle of Christian living is not according to what men say but according to what the Bible says. If we find out the principle of Christian living from the examples and patterns set forth in the Bible, we will know how to behave ourselves in our family life and social life. Therefore, in our daily living, in matters great or small, we should search the Bible and find out what it says that we should do. The most blessed and wise people are those who know the Bible. The Bible is the one book in the world that can best enlighten people. We have many problems that we cannot resolve, but once we bring them to the Bible, they are readily resolved.

A CHRISTIAN HAVING THE CHURCH

Third, a Christian has the church. This refers to the church which has been recovered back to the beginning, back to the condition of the early churches where things were not done according to man's methods but only according to the Bible. A Christian cannot be a Christian by himself alone; he must be in the church and have the church life. If a tree stands alone on a high mountain, it cannot easily remain standing; if it grows in a dense forest, it cannot easily topple. Satan loves to see Christians in isolation. A normal Christian in a locality should take the ground of that locality as the sphere in which to meet and serve with the saints there. As long as those saints are meeting according to the Bible and according to the practice of the early churches, they represent the church in that locality. Therefore, all Christians in that locality must be included. Hence, when we have problems, we should inquire not only of the Lord and of the Bible, but we should also inquire of the saints. We should look into the matters with them to find some solutions either in the church meetings or through private fellowship. This is truly a great protection and a proper help to us.

Sometimes because a church is big, it is not easy for the leading brothers to make decisions in matters related to the brothers and sisters. Normally when someone has a problem, he likes to seek advice from men of integrity. In the church, we are so blessed that the Lord has given us a group of devout believers. If someone in the church in Taipei is thinking about going to Taichung, he should ask where the church in Taichung meets. He should go only to a place where Christ, the Bible, and the church are. The church is a great help to us. Sometimes we may feel that the meetings are too long and boring and do not realize that they are actually a great blessing to us. Other times when we are away from home, we have no opportunity to meet with the saints for fellowship and for breaking of bread, and we feel a void within; we truly miss the saints and long to break bread with them. This kind of feeling is similar to the feeling we have when we are short of food. Every day we take our meals, but we do not realize the preciousness of food until we have been starved for three days. When we are hungry, we are not particular about what we are going to eat; at such a time everything is good to our taste.

If we were put in a place without a church, after one month of not having Christ and two months of not having our fellow Christians, we would eventually have a sense that it is the most miserable place. Sometimes just a simple love feast for fellowship can bring us a sense of sweetness. This is what the church affords us. Perhaps some will say that they can meet in their home by themselves. This may be true, but the taste will be different because the church is missing. Please remember that the church is a great matter and has a tremendous supply. Let me use myself as an illustration. I am a person who speaks for God. If you were to put me in the mountains for a month, when I come down from the mountains, I would no longer have anything to preach. However, in the church after I speak today, I have more to speak tomorrow, and after speaking tomorrow, I have still more to speak the day after tomorrow. I can never exhaust my speaking because in the church there is a rich source.

All those who speak for God know the preciousness of the church. All the riches of the church issue from the church and are transfused back to the church. The newly saved ones may not fully understand this word but all those saints who have experienced the church life have this kind of experience. Many times we do not know what to say or do but through the church and through our being joined with the Spirit in us, we have the words and the leading to press forward. Therefore, whenever we touch the church, we touch a great matter; this will affect the way we take for our entire Christian life.

A CHRISTIAN HAVING FELLOW CHRISTIANS

Fourth, in addition to Christ, the Bible, and the church, a Christian must have Christians other than himself. This means that a Christian should have at least one or two other brothers or sisters to be his spiritual companions. As Christians, we should not be independent; rather, we should always have six or seven spiritual companions. Among them, some should be older than we are in physical age while others should be older than we are in spiritual years; they are to be our best friends throughout our life. Our growth before the Lord is due to their help and support. Not long ago an older brother went to be with the Lord. We had known each other for twenty years. However, we were not worldly friends; rather, we lived before the Lord with a love for one another. When he was alive, whenever I had an important matter, I would always consult with him; likewise, he would consult with me about everything. There were many occasions when I would talk things over with him rather than with my wife; and in like manner, he would discuss things with me and not necessarily with his wife. In our consultations with one another, we truly experienced the Lord's presence and blessing. The Lord can testify for us that a great part of my time before the Lord was spent with this brother.

Every Christian must have spiritual companions. In the church a brother should seek out one or two brothers while a sister should look for one or two sisters to be their spiritual companions. However, we should be wary of such a relationship turning into a mere friendship or social interchange. Love is proper, but intimacy is not. Although intimacy may not be a sin, please remember that intimacy deadens our spirit and causes us to lose the Lord's presence. Forgive me for saying that the sisters are especially prone to go one step beyond the proper limit in their contact and fellowship with each other and sometimes even to the extent that they lose the simplicity in the Lord. Do not forget that there should be a limit—the cross. Once you go beyond the limit and your relationship with the saints becomes a friendship, then you must reject it. Nevertheless, it is of necessity that a Christian has some fellow Christians as his spiritual companions, just as Moses had Joshua, David had Jonathan, and Daniel had his three companions. In the New Testament, Peter had James, and Paul had Timothy; they all had companions in the Lord. Every Christian should have some spiritual companions in the church. Then he will become a strong, rejoicing, and proper Christian.

CHAPTER THREE

A BASIC KNOWLEDGE OF THE BIBLE

As saved ones, we should at least have a basic knowledge concerning certain matters, such as, there is God, Jesus is our Savior, we are sinners, our sins have been forgiven, and we have the Lord's life in us. In addition, we should further know how the Bible came into existence, how it was handed down, how it was translated, and what its functions are. We should also know who Christ is. Is He God or is He a man? What was He in the past, and what will He be in the future? Not only so, we should know the development of Christianity on earth. What is the "old religion"? What is the "new religion"? What is the Catholic, or Roman Catholic, Church? What is the Greek Orthodox, or the Eastern Orthodox, Church? We need to have a basic knowledge of all these matters.

THE ORIGIN OF THE BIBLE
The Bible Being the Word of God

Christians all acknowledge that the Bible is God's word, God's speaking. Not only so, the Bible is God's speaking to man through human language. The Bible comes out of God and is God's own speaking, yet God speaks by words that are intelligible to man. Because man understands only the human language, and because God desires to speak to man, God must use a language which man can understand. We may compare this to the way we use the appropriate language to express our ideas to a foreigner; even though we speak in a foreign language, the content is still our thoughts.

There are several great matters in the universe. The first matter is God's creation of heaven and earth, which is an evidence of God's existence. That God created all things proves

His existence. Everyone recognizes that the creation of the universe, the existence of the universe, is a great miracle. The universe is so mysterious and so great, yet it came into being through creation and is upheld and borne by Christ. This great matter proves the existence of God.

The second great matter in the universe is God's speaking. God, indeed, created the universe; however, if God merely uses the universe to prove His existence, it would be difficult for man to fathom and believe. Therefore, God came in to speak to man. The creation of God is the verification of God, whereas the speaking of God is the explanation of God, the making known of God Himself by His speaking. For example, I have something in my pocket, but if I do not say anything about it, then you will have to make all kinds of guesses as to what it is. Some might be partially right and others might be totally wrong, but no one can be absolutely correct. However, once I explain what it is, then no one needs to guess; everyone will know what it is.

The Bible Being the Explanation of God

In the same way, the Bible is an explanation. The universe is the creation of God, whereas the Bible is the word of God, the explanation of God. The creation is God's work, and the word of God is His explanation. His word clearly tells us where the universe came from, what its course is, and where it is going. It even tells us in detail where man came from and where he is going. This is the Bible. Anyone who really knows the Bible will confess that it is the word spoken by God to reveal Himself, the universe and all of creation, and even the relationship of mankind with God.

God is a speaking God; He reveals Himself to man by His speaking. Those who do not know God might say that everything is really a mystery. Those who know God, however, can understand His revelation because they have the Spirit within and the Bible without. The universe is laid open to them, and the matters of the universe are as clear as crystal. If God had never spoken to mankind, then we would not know how to go on while we are living on earth. Hebrews 1:1-2a says, "God, having spoken of old in many portions and in many ways to the fathers in the prophets, has at the last of these days spoken to us in the Son." God spoke to the fathers in the ancient times. Now He is speaking to us. Moreover, God does not only speak, but He speaks continually. This is truly a sweet and wonderful thing.

The Bible Being Inspired by God

Perhaps some may ask, How can the Bible be the word of God? Was the Bible not written by men? This is not difficult to explain. For example, when someone telephones you from abroad and you hear his voice through the receiver, would you say that the voice is the voice of the receiver? We all know that the voice in the receiver comes from someone who is outside the receiver but speaks through the receiver. Apparently the Bible is the word of men; actually, it is the speaking of God in and through men. Second Timothy 3:16 says, "All Scripture is given by inspiration of God" (KJV). In Greek, *given by inspiration of God* means "God-breathed." The Scripture is the word of God breathed into men and then written down by men. It is God's thoughts being written into men and then spoken out by men. We may use the record player as an illustration. The voice is breathed out by the singer, stored onto a record, and then it is played back through the record player. We all know that the voice and the words stored on the record are exactly the same as the voice and the words uttered by the singer. It was the same in the beginning when God breathed out His thoughts to be received into men and then spoken out by men.

Every writer of the Scripture would reverently confess that what he wrote was not his own word but God's word. In the Old Testament, it is frequently mentioned that men were inspired by God. Balaam, who was an evil prophet, originally intended to curse the Israelites, but it was not up to him. Whenever he opened his mouth, he spoke words of blessing instead of words of cursing. Those words were not what he had intended to say; rather, they were beyond what he had expected (Num. 23—24). In this way, we can understand the meaning of being inspired by God. God spoke through men by giving them inspiration. This means that the Spirit of God came upon men and wrote the word of God through them. The Bible was written in this way.

The Bible Originating from God

There were approximately forty writers of the Bible. Among them, some were men of noble birth, such as King David; some were lowly men, such as Peter; some were shepherds, such as Amos; some were highly educated, such as Moses; some were men of great wisdom, such as Paul; and some were very simple, such as John. Some lived in palaces and some were in the wilderness; some were in Judea and some were in Arabia. They had different styles, they were in different places, and they wrote at different times, yet when their writings were put together, these writings formed the complete Bible with a consistent line of thought. This shows that the Bible truly came out of the inspiration of God. God first wrote a portion through Moses, then after a period of time, wrote another portion through Isaiah; later He wrote through Jeremiah and still later through Daniel; then finally He wrote through John. There were at least forty writers, yet they all wrote under the divine inspiration over a period of more than 1500 years. The first book was written by Moses around 1500 B.C.; the last book was written by the apostle John around A.D. 94-96, 1500-1600 years after the first book. The entire Bible consists of sixty-six books. These books were written in many different places, such as Palestine, Rome, and Ephesus. However, although they were written in so many places, over such an extended period of time, and through so many hands, after they had been compiled together, they formed the complete Bible, in which all the thoughts are consistent. This is full proof that the Bible truly originates from God.

THE TRANSMISSION OF THE BIBLE

It is amazing that the Bible could be transmitted to us. The first book of the Old Testament—Genesis—was written about 1500 B.C., and the last book—Malachi—was written about 400 B.C. In other words, the Old Testament was already completed in 400 B.C. After the Lord Jesus came, in His preaching He often quoted the words of the Old Testament. This is proof that at His time the Old Testament had already been completed.

When the Lord Jesus was on earth, since printing had not yet been invented, the Bible had to be copied by hand on sheepskin. The Jewish scribes were very reverent in making copies of the Scriptures. History tells us that they wrote on sheets made from the choicest sheepskin and exercised the greatest possible care in copying. They counted not only the words, but every letter in every line. If an incorrect letter was found, the whole copy was rejected. It is said that the writers also had to pronounce each word aloud before writing it. They were required to wipe their pen before writing the name of God in any form, and to wash their whole body before writing *Jehovah*. This shows how much they revered the holy Scriptures. After the Lord Jesus had departed the world, the apostles were inspired to write the New Testament. By A.D. 100 the entire New Testament had been completed. In the second century, the God-fearing people often cited the words of the New Testament in their writings. This proves that within a hundred years after the Lord's departure, the New Testament was already there.

The Old Testament was written in Hebrew, the ancient language of the Jews. The following four passages, however, were written in Aramaic: Jeremiah 10:11; Daniel 2:4—7:28; Ezra 4:8—6:18; and Ezra 7:12-26. These portions contain records of the events related to the Babylonians, who used the Aramaic language, so they were written in Aramaic and not in Hebrew. The Chaldeans also adopted the Aramaic language. At the time of the Lord Jesus, many Jews still used the Aramaic language. By that time the Roman Empire had already captured the land of Israel. When the Roman Empire conquered all the surrounding areas of the Mediterranean Sea and spread the Greek culture to all those places, the Greek language became the common language of the Roman Empire of that day. Hence, the apostles used Greek for the writing of the New Testament.

The Bible in common use today, however, was not translated from the original manuscripts because they have all been lost. According to the researchers of the ancient manuscripts, the oldest manuscripts that have been discovered are from the third and fourth centuries after Christ. In other words, the oldest manuscripts are only 1500 to 1600 years old. Although the originals are no longer in existence, three early manuscripts still exist. These have been considered to be three among the fifty copies of the Bible which were made through an edict issued by Emperor Constantine in A.D. 330.

Of these three manuscripts, the oldest and most complete copy is known as the *Vaticanus* manuscript and is being kept in the Vatican Library. It was done around A.D. 350 and was discovered over 500 years ago. The second copy, which was beautifully written, is the *Sinaiticus* manuscript. In 1844 it was discovered by Dr. Tischendorf, a renowned German scholar, in a monastery at the foot of Mount Sinai. Later, it was deposited in the Royal Library of Russia until 1933, when it was sold to the British Museum in London for 100,000 pounds sterling. The third copy is the *Alexandrinus* manuscript. It was presented to King Charles I in 1628 by Cyril Lucar, a Greek patriarch of Alexandria, and is also being kept in the British Museum, London. Thus, of these three ancient manuscripts, two are in London and one is in the Vatican.

THE TRANSLATION OF THE BIBLE

Around 400 B.C. all the books of the Old Testament had been completed. By 300 B.C. the Jews who dwelt in Egypt, in the city of Alexandria, had begun to translate the Bible from Hebrew to Greek. The five books of Moses were finished around 270 B.C., and then the remaining books of the Old Testament were translated in the subsequent one hundred fifty years. This became the earliest translation of the Hebrew Bible. According to the *Letter of Aristeas,* this translation was done by seventy-two scholars, all of whom were experts both in Hebrew and in Greek; hence, it was called the *Septuagint,* which is the earliest translation of the Bible. Later when the Roman Empire unified the areas surrounding the Mediterranean Sea, some began to translate the Bible into Latin, but their translations were in a crude vernacular style and contained many absurdities. In A.D. 384 the church father

Jerome undertook the revision of the Latin New Testament; his work of retranslating was completed in A.D. 388. The Latin translation of the Old Testament from the original Hebrew was finished by A.D. 404. This version was later called the *Vulgate,* which itself is a Latin word, meaning "made common." Hence, it is also known as the Latin "common" version and is still being used by the Roman Catholic Church today.

At the time of the Reformation, the primary work of Luther was to translate the Bible into German. This marked the beginning of the Bible's being widely translated into different languages. As to the English Bible, John Wycliffe was the first to translate the *Vulgate* into English. Afterward William Tyndale and a few others also undertook the translation work. However, due to the great differences reflected in the various versions, in 1604, King James I of England established a Bible translation committee and assembled fifty scholars to undertake the translation work. Subsequently, in 1611 the authorized English version, the King James Version, was published. This version was gradually accepted by Christians as the standard version of the English Bible because of its fluency in the English language and its faithfulness to the original language. Later in 1870, due to the progress made in research on the original languages and the old manuscripts, nearly a hundred British and American scholars formed a committee to revise the King James Version. The revision of the New Testament was completed in 1881 while that of the Old Testament was done in 1885. This translation is known as the Revised Version. After the completion of its work, the committee transmitted all the texts from England to America by telegraph. Then after further revisions in vocabulary were made, another edition was published in 1901 in the United States and is known as the American Standard Version. Because this translation was very faithful to the original text, about ninety-five percent of the content of subsequent Chinese versions conformed to this version.

The work on the Chinese translation also underwent a long process. The earliest traceable work, carried out in the thirteenth through the sixteenth centuries, was the translation of the New Testament and the book of Psalms by some Catholic priests in China, including John of Monte Corvino and Matteo Ricci. Then in 1807, Robert Morrison went to China to preach the gospel. During his stay, he translated the Bible into the Chinese language with the help of a Chinese helper by the name of Liang Ya-fa. This version was published in 1823. Subsequently, various Chinese Bible versions came off the press, but nearly all of them were in classical Chinese. In 1885, John Griffith, an evangelist who preached the gospel in the northeastern region of China, used the semi-vernacular Chinese style to translate the New Testament. Then in 1889 a New Testament, entirely in vernacular Chinese, was officially published. A year later, a joint convention of the missionary societies of various Protestant denominations in China was held in Shanghai. During that time, there were ardent discussions about the translation of the Bible into Chinese. As a result, a committee of seven scholars was formed to be responsible for the undertaking. After twenty-eight years of laboring, in 1919, the entire Union Version was completed using the official Chinese language. The literary style was beautiful, far surpassing all other versions. Hence, it is still widely used today. In 1939, after some revisions, it became known as the Mandarin Union Version or simply the Union Version.

THE WAY TO READ THE BIBLE

Throughout the generations Christians have had many ways of reading the Bible. Some of the ways require much time and effort but produce little result, while other ways likewise require much time and effort but yield no result at all. However, one way that is worth trying is to read the Bible once a year. Daily read one chapter of the New Testament and three chapters of the Old Testament; this is to read four chapters a day. In this way the Bible can be read through once in a year. It is best to read the New Testament in the morning and the Old Testament during the day. This way is even more necessary for the new believers. After you rise up every morning, before doing anything else, you should pray and read the Bible. This does not require a great amount of time. Normally people think that they do not have enough hours in a day, but if we allot time to read the Word and pray, we will gain the benefit of redeeming our time. More importantly, this will cause us to be nourished and supplied every day; we will not only increase in knowledge but also grow in life.

Furthermore, when you read the Bible, first you need to follow its sequence. Read the Old Testament starting with Genesis and the New Testament with Matthew, reading both parts in parallel and following the sequence chapter by chapter and verse by verse. In this way you can easily finish reading the Bible once a year. Second, there is no need to seek for a deep understanding. Your seeking for deeper understanding may actually become a hindrance. When you are just beginning to read the Bible, the more you read, the better. Do not just read more chapters but more books. Third, there is the need to pay attention to the facts or the summary of each chapter. For example, Matthew chapter one tells us two things: first, the genealogy of Christ; second, the birth of Christ. It is sufficient to remember these facts.

Fourth, receive inspiration from each chapter you have read. From that chapter there may be a sentence or a few verses that touch you very much. You should meditate on them, pray over them, and memorize them. For example, Matthew 1:21 says, "And she will bear a son, and you shall call His name Jesus, for it is He who will save His people from their sins." If you are moved by this word "for it is He who will save His people from their sins," then you can pray, "Lord Jesus, I ask You to wash away whatever sins are still in me. Lord, I am sinful. Save me from my sins." In doing so, the benefits you receive daily will be immeasurable. If you cannot understand a certain portion, do not be anxious to understand it right away. In time, when you come back to that portion, you will spontaneously understand more and eventually understand it thoroughly.

If we read the Bible in this way, the more we read, the more we will be helped and the more our spiritual life will grow. This is a continuous cycle of cause and effect. In addition, when reading, it is best to go through the Old Testament at a faster pace; just try to remember the facts and this will be good enough. Holidays and vacations are the best times to read the Bible. During such days, we should spend more time to read and memorize the Scriptures. This will stabilize our Christian life and keep us from slipping. When we come to the Bible, we are coming before God; hence, each time we read the Bible we are refreshed. Many of us love to read magazines and newspapers. However, that kind of reading can only increase our worries; it cannot refresh us. When we read the Bible, however, we are always refreshed. This is just like a glass being washed in water; even if it is empty, at least it is clean.

Someone may ask, "How can I read the Bible? My memory is poor, so I cannot remember anything I read." Whether we can remember what we read is another matter. The primary purpose of our reading the Bible is that we may be nourished and enlightened so that we may have strength for our living, light for our way, and growth for our spiritual life. May we begin immediately to practice this.

CHAPTER FOUR

THE CONTENT OF THE CHURCH

The history of Christianity, as an account of the course of Christianity on earth, tells us about its development on earth for the last two thousand years and its condition today before the whole world. We need to have the knowledge of such a history so that we may understand the condition of Christianity. We also need to receive revelation from the Word of God to see what the church is that God desires.

THE CHURCH BEING THE SUM TOTAL OF GOD IN ALL THE BELIEVERS

What is the church? What is the content of the church? Probably many Christians have difficulty answering these questions. Some say that the church is the enlargement of the principle of Christ. Then what is the principle of Christ? The principle of Christ is that God is added into man. Hence, the church is the sum total of God in all those who have God.

THE CHURCH BECOMING DEFORMED THROUGH HUMAN HANDS

The church has one unique characteristic—simplicity. Such a characteristic cannot be found in any worldly society or organization. In the beginning the church was brought forth in a simple way without human hands. Today, related to time, the church has been on the earth for two thousand years; related to space, the church has spread over the whole globe. In the process, however, the church has also become deformed through human hands.

In the course of two thousand years, the church, which has

spread across the Eastern and Western Hemispheres and has now come into our midst, is no longer in her original form. Just consider if an object were to pass through my hands and your hands and then through another two hundred hands, what would become of it? Would its shape not be altered? We must believe in Christ and in the Bible, but we must not believe in Christianity in its present form. Christ is unchangeable. Throughout the centuries many have tried to change Christ, yet Christ remains unchanged. Before World War I there was a strong wind in Europe attempting to alter Christ. This wind quickly blew over to America, and after World War I this wind also blew into China. Nevertheless, ultimately Christ could not be altered. Similarly, the Bible is also unchangeable. However, so-called Christianity has been altered so drastically that it is beyond recognition.

A QUESTION MARK ON CHRISTIANITY

We must have absolute faith in Christ and in the Scripture. We must put a question mark, however, on every item and every aspect of Christianity. For example, when we see a chapel, we have to ask, Did the original church have such a thing? When we hear the clanging of church bells, we must ask, Did the original church have such an item? When we see the cross, we also have to ask, Did the original church have such a thing? When we see the clergy, all the more we must ask, Was there such a thing in the early church? Concerning everything related to the present condition of Christianity, we should earnestly question if these things indeed existed in the beginning. There are so many items in Christianity that are not according to the Bible. In the genuine church, however, everything should be according to the Bible.

I was saved when I was still in school. For a year before I was saved, I was a so-called church member. After I was saved, I began to diligently read the Bible. Gradually I found out that in the church where I was there were many practices which could not be found in the Bible. Therefore, I had many questions within me about those matters. Whenever I had the opportunity, I would go to see the pastor or some other leading ones in the church to discuss those matters. However, the more I talked with them, the more I felt that something was wrong. They did not have many of the things that are found in the Bible, yet they had so many other things that are not found in the Bible. They had altered almost everything except the fundamental truths such as Jesus being our Savior and Jesus being the true God. This is why we must put a question mark on today's Christianity.

THE CHURCH NOT BEING
A PHYSICAL BUILDING FOR WORSHIP

The characteristic of the church in the beginning was her simplicity. The church today, having been altered, is no longer so simple. According to the principle of simplicity, when the early church was raised up, she did not have many of the things that we see in Christianity today, not even a physical place for worship, such as a cathedral—something so greatly valued today. The believers met at times in public squares, sometimes in the portico of Solomon, and at other times in their homes. Basically, there were no chapels or cathedrals. The concept of building physical places for worship did not exist until the degradation of the church under Roman Catholicism. The Roman Catholic Church brought the heathen customs and practices, including idolatry, into Christianity. Those who are knowledgeable about architecture all agree that the best buildings and structures in Europe are the cathedrals. It is reported that St. Peter's Cathedral in the Vatican was built at a cost of 90,000,000 pounds sterling, which is equivalent to several times that in dollars. This shows how highly regarded the cathedrals are in degraded Christianity.

The temple in the Old Testament was a physical building, and the temples or shrines of the Gentile idols were also physical structures. The holy temple was considered the best building structure among the Jews. The former temple was torn down, and it took forty-six years for the latter one to be built. Likewise, in China the best architecture in every place is also seen in the temples or shrines. However, when the church was first raised up, the worship of God was "neither in this mountain nor in Jerusalem" but "in spirit"

(John 4:21, 23). God cares only for our spirit. Thus, the Bible tells us that, individually, our body is the temple of the Holy Spirit. This means that God dwells in us (1 Cor. 6:19; Eph. 2:22). Corporately, the church is God's house, God's dwelling place. This means that God dwells in the church (1 Tim. 3:15). Therefore, the church is not a physical building for religious worship.

According to man's religious concept, a house used for church meetings is different from any ordinary house. Once I met a group of believers in Tientsin who called their meeting place the "holy assembly hall." I wondered if these people would not also call their homes "holy residences." Surely, a meeting hall and a regular house are different, but the difference is only in what they are being used for and not in whether they are holy or common. When the Lord began His recovery in China, Christians were raised up to take the way of the recovery in many major cities. At that time there was a group of young believers who were studying medicine in Ch'i-Lu University. After they had seen the light of the Lord, they loved Him fervently. Since they were students who lived in dormitories, they did not have a home or a place to meet. Thus, they held their first Lord's table in a cemetery. They placed the bread and the cup on a table used for offering sacrifices, and in this way they worshipped and remembered the Lord. All those who attended that meeting testified that they had never touched the reality of heaven or sensed the loveliness of the Lord as much as during that particular time.

THE CHURCH BEING NOT A PHYSICAL BUILDING BUT A SPIRITUAL BUILDING

The church is really simple. She is so simple that it seems she has nothing with respect to rules or regulations. Today, however, it seems that we cannot break the bread or worship the Lord unless we have a piano and a table. Please remember that this is a degraded and deformed situation. Someone may say that in the Catholic Church the cathedrals are imposing, the sacred songs are solemn, and the bishops are awe-inspiring. It has never occurred to him that these are items in a deformed situation. In contrast, there was nothing attractive outside or inside of the meeting hall of the church in Shanghai, yet every time there was a meeting, the hall was full. One time, two overseas Chinese attended a meeting there and were greatly astonished. One of them said, "I saw many places of worship in America, but they were never filled. I never imagined that when I came back to my homeland I could see people packed into such an unattractive place." It was marvelous to him but not to us because the early church was the same way—considering the physical things as nonessential.

As children of God, we must realize that all physical things will eventually be destroyed. We should build only the things that are spiritual. Degraded Christianity always likes to show people a grand piano, a beautiful pulpit, and an exquisite façade. We should not be like this. The church does not necessarily receive more of God's blessings by having a splendid building. Rather, when the church has the presence of God with His life, power, and strength, this is really God's blessing. Sometimes the believers have a desire to meet outdoors, but some are concerned about not having a podium or a piano. Actually, in the beginning the church did not have these things. Physical things are not essential because what we are building is not something physical but something spiritual for people to be strengthened from within. This is God's intention.

THERE BEING NO HIERARCHY IN THE CHURCH

Furthermore, in the early church there was no hierarchy. Yet today in many Christian organizations there is a class called the clergy. Is this according to the Bible? You can serve God, and I also can serve God. We all can serve God. Is there any difference between your service and my service to God? We may have different functions and points of emphasis, but essentially your service and mine should not be different. If we all intend to attain God's original goal, every one of us should serve God (1 Pet. 2:9).

In the early church, every believer was a serving one. Before they were saved, they lived for mammon, but from the day they were saved, they were separated from the world by

the Lord. They still had their occupations, but their occupations were only for their livelihood. Their primary occupation
was to serve God. We must be like the early believers if we
intend to serve God. Our job should become our secondary
occupation, merely for us to make a living. We no longer live
on the earth to make a living for ourselves but to serve God.
The early apostles and disciples all lived this way.

THE DEVELOPMENT OF THE HIERARCHY

In A.D. 313, Constantine made Christianity the state religion and strongly promoted it. He encouraged the Romans to
join the church and promised them rewards. Basically, those
who joined the church for rewards were not regenerated or
saved and therefore could not serve God. They came into
Christianity, but Christ did not come into them. They had not
been saved by God to come out of the world; rather, they were
still in union with the world. When the number of such ones
increased, some of them decided to bring the Judaic system
and practice into Christianity. In Judaism, not everyone could
serve God; only the priests could. The professing Christians
brought the Jewish priestly system into Christianity so that
they could continue their worldly living without caring for the
spiritual things. All spiritual matters were entrusted to the
priests. In the Catholic Church the priests were called
"fathers." The so-called Catholic fathers are equivalent to the
priests in Judaism, and the long robes which they wear are
the same as the robes of the Old Testament priests.

During the time of the Reformation, the reforms carried
out by Luther were very limited. In fact, the Protestant
churches inherited many traditions from the Roman Catholic
Church. The Catholic Church had priests; the Protestant
churches had pastors. Many of the Protestant churches were
called state churches. For example, the Anglican Church, or
the Church of England, was established as a state church
with its pastors and bishops receiving salaries from the gov-
ernment. Even today, when the king or queen of England is
crowned, the archbishop has to lay hands on him or her.

When the Episcopalian Church spread to China, it was
still a state church and still had its clergy, which was copied

from the priestly system of the Roman Catholic Church. Later, in Protestantism there were the private churches. Some Christians saw the truth in the Bible concerning baptism—that a person should be baptized after believing in the Lord. Others saw that the church should be administered by the elders. Consequently, those who were in favor of baptism formed the Baptist church while those who approved of the administration of the church by the elders formed the Presbyterian church. Later John Wesley was raised up by the Lord, and subsequently the Wesleyan church was formed. All these so-called churches have a pastoral system. Up to the present, in the Roman Catholic Church the priests still handle the sacred duties and serve God on behalf of the common people. The Protestant state churches have their bishops while the private churches have their pastors. Such a concept of a clergy-laity system seriously damages people and hinders them from serving God.

THE SERVICE OF GOD BEING A MATTER FOR ALL BELIEVERS

In the Lord's recovery there are no pastors; instead, we are all brothers (Matt. 23:8-11). The believers address each other as brothers and sisters. If a brother among us is serving God, then we should all be serving God. Sometimes in the matter of visitation a brother would say, "It is best for So-and-so to visit that person because then that person will definitely be saved." On the one hand, the brother who says this shows that he cares for the souls of people, and we should be joyful about this. On the other hand, why does he not go to visit and preach the gospel to that one? When he goes, he may not be able to preach the word clearly, but he should go again and again. And after many visits, he could even ask someone to go with him. In short, there is no class among us. We all can and should participate in every aspect of the service of God. A person who is saved has God's life in him and can fellowship with God. Therefore, he should serve God. All of us, not just a few, should participate in the service of God.

What is degraded Christianity? In degraded Christianity everyone cares only for his own affairs while turning over the service of God to a few pastors or clergymen. Just as people ask lawyers to handle their lawsuits and ask doctors to cure their sicknesses, so Christians ask pastors to serve God on their behalf. This is absolutely wrong. In the initial church there was not such a practice. Neither Peter nor Paul practiced this. Peter would have said, "I am your brother," and so would Paul. What is the degradation of the church? If there are eighteen hundred saints in the church but only two to three hundred are serving God, that is the degradation of the church. Then, what is the normal condition of the church? The normal condition of the church is that if there are eighteen hundred saints, all of them are serving God. They all participate in the services of preaching the gospel, praying, and praising. They are all brothers serving together before God.

Some of the saints have asked me to preside over their wedding meeting which was to be held in the meeting hall. I told them that the initial church did not have such a practice and that perhaps they could have their wedding meeting in the house of a brother or sister who has a large living room. Although I have been serving God for such a long time and have come to know thousands of believers, I have never yet officiated at anyone's wedding. This kind of intermediary service is a degraded situation and should be removed from our midst. This is why during our meetings, many times I like to sit at the back. Sometimes, at the Lord's table, even though some of the prayers are very weak, I would not utter a word. I simply keep a position—that we do not have a pastor or someone presiding over the meeting among us. When I am on the podium and God gives me a word to release, I dare not shrink back, because that is my ministry. However, the Lord's table is for all the saints to worship God, so everyone must function.

When someone is sick in our family, especially if he is very ill, we usually ask the saints who are considered to be more spiritual to pray for the sick one. This type of action generally has two implications. First, it implies that we believe that we ourselves are incapable of praying this kind of prayer for healing. Second, it implies that due to our superstition we think that this kind of prayer will be more effective if it is offered by those who are more spiritual. We must all be clear that in the church there is no one who rules and there is no one who specializes in prayer. Every one of us can pray and should pray. The degradation of Christianity resulted in the so-called clergy. The Catholic Church has become so great that she has a pope who has become the king of kings so that his commands cannot be altered. Although the pope cannot rule the whole earth, he does rule over the Catholic Church throughout the whole world. The Lord Jesus said that we must not be like the Gentiles who have rulers and also that whoever wants to be great among us should do the most menial things (Matt. 20:25-27). In the cleaning service in some of the meeting halls, when the responsible brothers clean the bathrooms, it is an encouragement to the saints because it shows that we are all brothers before God and thus there should be no hierarchy among us. If we bring hierarchy into the church, the church will become a society. We can hire servants in our homes; in the church, however, there are no hired servants. We have bosses over us in a society, but not in the church. The normal church, which is very simple, has only brothers and sisters; there is nobody else.

Often people ask, "How do I join the church? What is the procedure for joining the church?" When a person prays and receives the Lord, that is the procedure and he is therefore already in the church. Please remember, whenever the church talks about procedures or regulations, then that church has already become degraded. The church is very simple, having only one God, one Lord, one Holy Spirit, and one Bible. This is the simplicity of the church—having no cathedrals, having no intermediary class, and giving no undue attention to wealth. Some people may ask, "Since the Lord has blessed you so much, why do you not build a grand cathedral with a steeple higher than all other cathedrals?" Peter said that he did not possess silver and gold (Acts 3:6). Paul said that he was naked and without a home (1 Cor. 4:11). The church does not have great wealth, and when the church has a little excess, it is distributed to the poor and the needy.

I already had a small family when I gave up my job to serve the Lord, and I can also testify that what the Lord gave me in one year far exceeded what I had before. Nevertheless, nothing we receive should be kept for our own enjoyment. We have many brothers and sisters who still do not have a place to live; they are still lacking in many things. Some of them ought to be resting in bed, yet for their livelihood they have to continue working. Moreover, there is a great deal of gospel work that requires expenses. Thus, we should not be rich before the Lord but live a simple church life, a life that is "as poor yet enriching many" (2 Cor. 6:10), just as Paul did.

CHAPTER FIVE

THE PECULIAR LIFE OF A CHRISTIAN

FOUR CHARACTERISTICS OF A CHRISTIAN

A Christian has four distinctive possessions: Christ, the Bible, the church, and fellow Christians. In addition, a Christian has four distinct characteristics: before men, he is peculiar; within himself, he is contradictory; before God, he takes his innermost part as the starting point; and in all things, he is led by God.

CHRISTIANS BEING A PECULIAR PEOPLE TO GOD

From the Scriptures we can see that according to God's will and ordination, as well as His salvation, a Christian is an extraordinary person. If a Christian is so ordinary and common that there is not the least bit of difference between him and any other human being, then something must be wrong with him. As a saved one with the life of God within him, a Christian has to be an extraordinary person. Titus 2:14 tells us that Christ "gave Himself for us that He might redeem us from all lawlessness and purify to Himself a particular [or, peculiar] people as His unique possession." This means that God saves us so that we may be a particular people as His unique, peculiar possession. This also has been our experience.

THE PECULIAR BEHAVIOR OF A CHRISTIAN

In the Scripture, the reference to a Christian's being "peculiar" has two meanings. First, it means that a Christian is peculiar in his outward behavior. Almost everyone has the sense that genuine Christians behave differently from the worldly people. We have often said that the world is a power-ful current. In such a current, people simply follow the flow in the world, even though they do not all follow the bad exam-ples to do bad things. However, a genuine Christian, having been saved, does not go with the flow in many situations; rather, he goes against the flow and is always going upward. Thus, he behaves differently from others and looks peculiar to them. For example, when some people want to go to a movie, it is peculiar if a Christian among them does not want to go. People in the world all go with the tide, but not the Christians, because they have received the Lord's salvation.

THE PECULIAR LIFE OF A CHRISTIAN

Second, that a Christian is "peculiar" means that within him he has a peculiar life with a peculiar nature. Although many Christians know that they have been saved, they do not know where the difference lies between them and the unbe-lievers. The greatest difference lies in the fact that Christians have the Lord's life within them. We all know that a certain life has a certain nature with certain innate functions. For example, the life of the fish has a distinctive nature which enables the fish to live in water. If we put a bird in the water, not only will it dislike the water, but even its life will be in danger. This is because birds do not have the innate ability to live in water. Birds fly in the air, whereas fish swim in water. The birds may consider the fish strange because the fish cannot fly in the air but can live only in water. Actually, this is being different. However, this difference is not merely in behavior; it is a difference in life. Fish live in water not because they are odd but because they have a life that enjoys staying in water and that is also able to stay in water. Simi-larly, everyone who believes in the Lord has His life, and this life has its nature, its innate ability, which causes him to be different from the unbelievers. Such a difference is higher and greater than the difference between the birds and the fish.

Giving Cheerfully

Let me illustrate this matter further. Before a person is saved, he is always happy whenever he receives something, regardless of whether he has received it as a gift, he has earned it, or he has obtained it by some unrighteous means. Have you ever experienced, however, that the joy of giving is much greater than the joy of receiving? Of course, we are joyful when someone gives us a sum of money or any material thing that delights us. This, however, is not our greatest joy. We experience the greatest joy when we give to others. I have had many such experiences. I have some amount of joy when someone has given me a gift. However, that joy is outward and not inward. On the other hand, when I offer help to the needy brothers and sisters by sending them gifts, that joy is beyond description. Many brothers and sisters have no joy because they are unwilling to give.

The life received by Christians has a special nature and character—cheerful giving. The Lord Jesus told a young man to sell all his possessions and follow Him (Matt. 19:21). John the Baptist also said, "He who has two tunics, let him share with the one who has none" (Luke 3:11). When the life of Christ came into us, the nature of cheerful giving also came into us. We can see how great our joy will be if we are willing to give some of our possessions to the poor. Honestly speaking, as Christians, we should voluntarily set aside some of our possessions and share them with the poor and the needy. If we practice this, we will definitely have the inner joy.

Suppose some brothers and sisters are in financial difficulties. When other brothers and sisters find out about this matter, they remember these needy ones before the Lord and provide some financial assistance to them in secret. You can just imagine what a joy it will be to the needy ones when they receive the supply. Then one day when these ones who received the supply find out that other brothers and sisters are having financial difficulties, they too will contribute a portion of their resources according to the Lord's leading. Their joy then will be far sweeter than their former joy. May we all have a taste of such sweetness.

Not Resisting

Furthermore, a Christian also has a nature that delights in yielding instead of resisting. In Matthew 5 the Lord Jesus tells us, "Whoever slaps you on your right cheek, turn to him the other also. And to him who wishes to sue you and take your tunic, yield to him your cloak also; and whoever compels you to go one mile, go with him two" (vv. 39-41). This is not merely a teaching; it is the nature of a Christian's life. For example, you may be engaged in a business with another brother, and when it comes time to settle accounts, you may get into an argument concerning some of the profits and dividends. Consider this: Are you happier when you are fighting for your share or when you willingly receive less? Suppose you and I are engaged in business. At the year-end settlement of accounts, you want to take fifty percent of the profits, and I want sixty percent because I believe that I put in more effort. Who has the joy in such a situation—you or I? In the end, neither of us has any joy. If, having enjoyed grace, you say to me, "Brother, you may have one hundred percent," then you will be joyful. And if I also say to you, "Brother, you may take all the profits," then I will also be filled with joy.

Once two brothers came to me because they had a dispute about some business dealings. Brother A said that Brother B was asking for too much money, while Brother B said it was Brother A who broke his promise because that was the sum agreed upon originally. They asked me to represent the church to settle the matter fairly. Therefore, I had some fellowship with the leading brothers and they all said, "This is totally unreasonable! How could a brother ask for more than his share from another brother? And how could a brother refuse to give what is due another brother?" They all agreed that the matter should be settled equitably but did not know how to proceed, so they consulted me. I said, "We should tell Brother A to give everything to Brother B, and we should also ask Brother B to give everything to Brother A." According to the teaching and the principle shown in the Bible, resisting one another does not issue in peace and joy.

Thus, when Brother A came to me, I said, "You have asked me to settle this matter fairly, and I feel that the best way of settlement is to go beyond fairness." He asked, "What do you mean by going beyond fairness?" I told him that it simply meant that he had to give everything to Brother B. Then he asked, "How could this be?" I said, "According to what you said, it is fair to give him thirty percent. If I instruct you according to your word, apparently I am helping you, but in reality I am doing you harm because you will lose your joy. On the other hand, if you give him all, you will have joy and your joy will be full." Upon hearing this, Brother A began to shed tears, though not tears of sorrow. Then he knelt down to pray and left rejoicing. When Brother B came, I also said to him, "We have to go beyond fairness. The Bible rightly says that when brothers contend with one another, what they gain is dung, and they will not have joy. As Christians, we should yield to others willingly. Whoever slaps us on our right cheek, we turn to him the other also. To be a Christian is to be able to turn the other cheek to be slapped. If you give him all, then you will overflow with joy." Upon hearing this, Brother B also knelt down to pray because he truly had the life of Christ.

Consider this: Who has joy—the one who strikes or the one who is struck? Christians are very peculiar. They rejoice in being struck but do not rejoice in striking others. This is why I told those two brothers that if we insist on being treated fairly, surely we will lose our joy. The life of Christians is a life of peace and joy. Whenever we contend with others, we have neither peace nor joy. If we are not like this, there may be two problems: either we are not saved or the life within us is not adequately manifested. The Bible tells us that it is more blessed to give than to receive (Acts 20:35). We have the inner joy when we delight in giving, more than in receiving.

Reluctant to Make a Show

Christians possess a life that is not only willing to give but also reluctant to make a show. For example, a sister who plays the piano may be invited to a recital. She performs excellently and is praised by everyone. Do you think she can rejoice when she goes home? Do you think she can kneel down and pray? Normally, she cannot go home with joy. She loses her inner joy as soon as people shower praises upon her. This is a marvelous thing. On the contrary, if she performs poorly, although she will feel dejected outwardly, when she goes home she can kneel down to pray and be filled with joy from the Lord. Being reluctant to make a show is a special nature of the extraordinary life of the Lord Jesus.

People in the world all like to make a show of themselves. Christians, however, are unique—they dislike making a display of themselves. For example, in the matter of rendering help to others, most people are eager to make it known to everyone. Christians, however, are reluctant to make it known and feel uncomfortable, even unhappy deep within, if it has been made known. Christians can praise God and be filled with joy only when they help others without making a public display and without being known.

Not Self-vindicating

Christians are in contrast to the worldly people in many respects because they have a life which is quite different from that of the worldly people. For example, when someone in the world has been wronged, he likes to vindicate himself and even issue a public statement so that he can make himself feel comfortable. However, if a Christian does likewise, he will lose his inner joy. This does not refer to his outward being but to his inner life, the life that is in all those who have Christ within. When a Christian suffers injustice, naturally he is not happy, but the life within him rejoices. He can tell the Lord, "Lord, someone has wronged me by telling lies about me, but You know me." He has the inner joy. This is to be a Christian. A Christian has an extraordinary life within him that gives him an extraordinary sense which leads him to live an extraordinary yet normal life. Such a life is unusual in the eyes of others but normal to the Christian himself. A Christian is normal in the sense that he is distinct from the worldly people and does not go along with the tide of the world because he has a peculiar life with a peculiar nature which is Christ Himself. Although many of his actions may seem unusual, and even strange or odd to others, they are manifestations of the peculiar life which he received when he was saved.

Obeying the Inner Sense of Life

Many Christians can neither pray nor offer thanksgiving in the meetings. With some, of course, it is due to their timidity and shyness, but with most Christians it is because their spirit is void of joy and is oppressed. They may feel that they have not committed any sin or done anything wrong, yet their spirit cannot be uplifted. The main reason is that they have formed the habit of neglecting the sense in their spirit. Some, when they feel that they are wrong do not ignore their feeling. Thus, they are released and freed in their spirit. When they come to the meetings, they can pray and testify spontaneously. A difficult matter with most Christians is that they have a peculiar life with a marvelous sense, yet in their circumstances, due to their disobedience, they are unable to live out a proper condition. As a result, they are Christians inwardly but do not live as Christians outwardly. They have Christ within but do not look like Christ without. This is all because although they have the sense within, they do not have the obedience without. Consequently, there is no difference between their living and the living of ordinary people.

It is difficult to find an honest person, a person who tells the truth one hundred percent. Nonetheless, a Christian should not lie. Once when I was going to Shanghai, I had to buy a ticket for baggage transportation. A porter told me, "Sir, your baggage is at least five kilograms, which is just a little over ten pounds, but you may declare that it is only two pounds." I felt uncomfortable because I could not lie, so I had my baggage weighed and ended up having to pay more freight charges. I knew that the porter wanted to help me, but he also wanted me to lie, so I could not listen to him. The porter stared at me angrily and said, "Do you not have a better place where you can use your money?" I simply smiled and did not say anything. He continued, "You are a foolish traveler. You simply do not know the rules of the game." I just stood there while he scolded me. Many times we will find ourselves in the same kind of situation. What should we do when we are being tempted? If I had cheated and said two pounds as suggested by the porter, I would have gained some monetary advantage but would have lost my inner joy. Therefore, we should rather keep our inner joy.

Another time, I was being interrogated by the Japanese authorities. The Japanese officer asked me, "Do you believe in God?" I said that I believed in God. Then he asked, "Who is greater, God or the Emperor of Japan?" I said that God is greater. Again, he asked, "Who is first, God or your country?" I said God is first. On the next day, before the officer began his interrogation, an interpreter came to see me and said, "Mr. Lee, since the Japanese officer wants you to say that your country is first, you should just say it. Why should you say that your God is first?" Saints, I hope that we can all see clearly that in such situations, the unbelievers are watching to see whether or not we are special and different from them. We can either tell the truth and suffer or not tell the truth and escape suffering. The worldly people and even the demons are waiting and watching to see how Christians face temptations.

Thus, we can see that some brothers and sisters cannot pray because they act contrary to the nature of the life within them. In their living they are always either lying to others or deceiving themselves. The cheapest thing in the world is lying. For instance, when a guest comes to see us, the most convenient way to refuse him is to ask someone else to tell him, "So-and-so is not home." In today's society, whether in hospitals, in schools, in offices, or in other organizations, it is very difficult to find people who do not lie. This is because lying is the easiest way to resolve a problem. All that is needed is to speak or write a few words as one sees fit. For example, people generally misstate their expenses when they go on business trips or misstate their overtime charges. In brief, there is something special in Christians. If we are Christians, we must be those who are genuine, proper, and on the right track so that we can live out the extraordinary nature of the life that is within us.

Those who have lived in Shanghai know that commuters there commonly practiced a dishonest thing. One time when I was returning from Cha-pei to Shanghai, before I reached my destination, someone who knew that I was getting off shortly approached me to ask for my ticket, so that he could make money by reselling it later to another commuter. I refused to give it to him because I had the conviction that I should not help him sin. Since I had repeatedly refused to give him my ticket, I almost had a clash with him one time when we met on the same electric car again. Another time, I met another person who was also trying to resell used tickets and who lectured me, "This company is British-owned. Since you are a Chinese, you ought to help your fellow Chinese to make some money from the British people." However, I have a peculiar life and nature within me. If I live and walk according to this life and nature, my spirit will be rejoicing, transcendent, and able to praise God; otherwise, I will feel depressed and lacking in joy.

Of course, it is convenient to ask someone to tell an unwelcome guest that we are not home, and there is also no great harm done to anyone when we help someone to reap some small gains by allowing him to resell our used ticket. Nevertheless, this will cause us to lose our inner joy. Although others will not find fault in us, our spirit will be deadened, and we will not be able to pray or give praises to God. In today's society very few can stay away from lying. It is precious that we are able not to lie. It is indeed difficult for us to be truthful in an environment which is filled with lies and hypocrisies. Nevertheless, Christians must all be clear that this is not just a teaching or a principle in the Bible; rather, it is the peculiar nature of the life in us. This requires our exercise and practice.

To go against the tide means that, for instance, even though everyone believes it is all right to lie, we are troubled within. Lying causes us to lose the ability to pray, praise, and fellowship. Others lie but we cannot—this is the distinction between us and the worldly people, and this is also our peculiarity. Therefore, the Lord often gives us a feeling which is different from the feeling of the worldly people. If we ignore the feeling we have from Christ and go along with the tide just like ordinary people, we have lost our way before God because we have lost the peculiar nature within us. However, if we obey that feeling and walk accordingly, we become a special people who are in this world as God's peculiar people upholding His marvelous testimony.

CHAPTER SIX

THE CONTRADICTION IN A CHRISTIAN

A CHRISTIAN HAVING CHRIST WITHIN

Christians have many special characteristics. The most evident is that they have Christ within them. This understanding must remain deeply and firmly in all Christians. Do not regard this matter as something ordinary; rather, consider it as something very special. We are saved ones before God because Christ has come into us. We grow in life because Christ has gained more ground in us. We are also knowledgeable, spiritual, and pious before God because Christ has increasingly gained ground in us. But how many Christians know thoroughly and clearly that Christ dwells in them and thus live in Christ? The fact is that not many Christians pay attention to this matter as much as God does.

From the day we were saved, God has wanted us to completely put ourselves aside. His intention is that we would let Christ live in us. In other words, formerly the Lord Jesus and we were two persons. The day we were saved, however, the Lord Jesus entered into us. Thus, He and we are no longer two but one. This is what God intends and hopes to accomplish. From the day we were saved, Christ and we are no longer two persons. Our desires, our thoughts, and our will have all been lost in Christ. Previously we lived and considered everything by ourselves. Christ was Christ, and we were we; He and we were two separate persons. The day we were saved, however, we received the Lord Jesus into us; indeed, He has come into us. Thus, we have become one with Him. This is God's desire. Unfortunately, this matter has long been neglected and even today has not been given sufficient attention by Christians.

Formerly the Lord Jesus and we were distinct and sepa-rate, but now we have become one. It used to be that Christ was Christ and we were we, but now Christ has come into us and has been joined with us. One thing happened immediately after He and we were joined together—we became Christians. Once we are saved and become Christians, we possess the life of Christ. However, even among the saved ones, there are two categories. One category consists of Christians who know that their sins have been forgiven, that Christ dwells in them, and that one day they will be with God forever. Moreover, they know that God answers their prayers and that the Spirit of God is moving in them. These Christians know that Christ is in them. The other category consists of Christians who are truly saved yet do not know that Christ dwells in them. If you ask them whether their sins have been forgiven, they will say that they have been forgiven and that they have the inner peace and joy that come with the forgiveness of sins. Further-more, they will tell you that they have been accepted and justified by God. They also know that one day when they die, they will be with God forever. However, one thing they do not know is that Christ lives in them.

Consider our own situation. We may have already been saved for a period of time, yet we think it strange when asked if Christ is living in us. We all know that our sins have been forgiven and that when we die we will be with God, but we may have never heard about Christ living in us. Perhaps some have told us about it, but their words quickly faded away. Regardless of how long we have been saved, while many of us have the assurance of our salvation, we do not necessarily know that Christ lives in us. This is a serious matter because the center of God's salvation is that Christ lives in man. Every saved one must clearly understand this matter.

Thus, Christians are those who have Christ in them. For example, we cannot call a cup a teacup unless it contains tea. A teacup must have tea in it. Before we were saved, we were merely human beings, but on the day we believed in the Lord and were saved, Christ came into us. Thus, we are no longer merely men; we are "Christ-men." A person who is saved has

Christ living in him. We must consider this an important matter.

GOD'S HOPE BEING THAT
CHRIST WILL GAIN MORE GROUND
IN THE SAVED ONES BY HIS LIVING IN THEM

God has a hope and a purpose in the saved ones. God's hope is that the more Christ lives in us, then the more He will gain ground in us, the more God's life will be expressed through us, and the more we will be lost in and assimilated by Him. God's intention is that Christ will gain us, saturate us, and completely assimilate us, so that we may be filled with Christ within and express Christ without. This is God's expectation. However, from the time we were saved, we have been preoccupied with improving ourselves, hoping that we will be better than before. For example, after having been saved, someone who previously sinned resolves not to sin again. Another one who likes to gossip decides to be more careful in his speaking. Still another one who has a bad temper is determined not to lose his temper again. These hopes are good but quite contrary to God's hope. This does not mean that we want to be good and that God wants us to be bad. Instead, this means that God is hoping for a goal which is higher and better than the goal we hope for.

THE SAVED ONES' HOPE BEING
TO BE ABLE TO IMPROVE THEMSELVES

God's hope is that the more Christ lives in us, the more He will be able to gain ground in us and be expressed through us. However, our hope is that the more Christ lives in us, the more we will be improved in ourselves. We have to see that there is a significant discrepancy between these two hopes. Every saved one hopes that God will grant him more strength to help him reform himself so that he can do good deeds. This is good from the human perspective, but those who know God realize that this is contrary to God's hope in us. When we live foolishly, not knowing what is good or bad, we do not have any expectation. But when we have been revived in the Lord, somehow we begin to have a desire to get rid of all our shortcomings. This is where the problem lies: God hopes that the more Christ lives in us, the more He will be able to gain ground, but our hope is that the more He lives in us, the more we will be able to improve ourselves. God hopes that Christ can have more ground in us, while we hope that we can improve ourselves; these two hopes are totally different.

GOD'S SALVATION BEING
FOR CHRIST TO ENTER INTO US

We have been saved, and Christ has entered into us; we have been lost in Him, and He has become one with us. Please consider: When we were saved, was it because we were merely subdued in our thoughts and preferences or because we were saved by the Lord Jesus? Since it is the Lord Jesus who has saved us, our thoughts and preferences must be dissolved in His thoughts and preferences, and our will and inclination must be dissolved in His will and inclination. What is God's salvation? God's salvation is that God wants our entire being, including our mind, emotion, and will, to be completely dissolved and lost in the Lord Jesus, just like sugar which has been dissolved in water is completely lost in the water. Now the two, the Lord and we, have become one and cannot be separated. This is to be a genuine Christian.

GOD'S SALVATION BEING A STEP-BY-STEP PROCESS

Do not think that God's salvation is simply to admonish people to do good. Rather, God's salvation is for us to be lost in Christ. From the day we were saved, God's salvation is simply the Lord Jesus Himself coming into us and being mingled with us. The Lord Jesus is in us as our salvation. He is saving us step by step until He saves us to the full extent. Our regeneration is the initial step of our being saved. We will be saved to the full extent when we are completely dissolved in Him. When our thoughts, insight, preferences, and disposition are completely dissolved in Christ, His insight becomes our insight, and His preferences become our preferences; then on that day we will enjoy God's salvation in full.

CHRISTIANS BEING FULL OF CONTRADICTIONS

Before the day comes when we fully enjoy God's complete salvation, our Christian life is a life of contradictions. We have said that Christians possess four things—Christ, the Bible, the church, and fellow Christians—and that Christians are also peculiar. But this is not all; Christians are also full of contradictions. When a person first becomes a Christian, he begins to experience a life of countless contradictions from morning to evening. Prior to his salvation, his inner being is consistent, without any ups and downs and without any conflicts. For example, he goes east if he wants to go east, and he goes west if he wants to go west; he does whatever he wants. However, strangely enough, from the day he is saved and becomes a Christian, he begins to experience inner contradictions. It seems that whenever he has a certain feeling, he will have another feeling, and the two feelings usually are contrary to one another.

If as a Christian a person does not experience contradictions, his being a Christian is questionable. For example, when you and another brother are discussing a certain matter, after saying just a few sentences, you have a sense that it is better not to say anything more. Thus, a contradiction arises from within you. In the early stage of salvation, a normal Christian is filled with contradictions; if this is not the case, perhaps he has not yet been saved. We all have this kind of experience. Whenever we love a certain person, a certain thing, or a certain matter beyond a certain degree, there arises from within us a feeling which limits and restricts us, causing us to resist that kind of love. This inner sense of disapproval gives rise to a contradiction in us.

There are times when a brother admonishes or prohibits us from doing a certain thing, yet we may find one, two, or even ten reasons why we should proceed. Although the brother has advised against it, we still think that we should do it. While we are rationalizing, however, the inner sense begins to oppose us. When we present our first reason, the inner sense refutes it. Then we present our second, third, fourth, and even tenth reason, but the inner sense refutes each one of

them. We say with our mouth that we still want to do it, but
something within us disagrees. There is a contradiction
within us.

Sometimes we submit inwardly but disobey outwardly,
and sometimes we submit outwardly but disobey inwardly.
Sometimes we may even say, "I sense within that I should not
say anything, but I also feel that I have to say something
in order not to let my opponent off lightly." This is the contradiction in a Christian. Here is a Christian who argues and
contends outwardly yet is met with disapproval inwardly.
Every Christian experiences this type of contradiction between
the inward sense and the outward action. Thus, when a Christian couple quarrels, there is no need for anyone to arbitrate.
When the argument is getting out of control, something
within them will bother them and not allow them to go on
quarreling. This kind of contradiction proves that they are
genuine Christians.

LOST IN CHRIST

Using myself as an example, I can say that my experience
of contradictions during the early years of my salvation was
unbearable. At the moment I finished dressing and was pre-
pared to go out, there came an inner sense that I should not
go, and then when I returned to my study room to read, there
came another sense that I should not read. I just did not know
what to do. This contradiction comes from two parties: we
ourselves and Christ in us. Perhaps according to our preference we want to visit a friend, but Christ says, "It is your
preference to visit your friend; I do not agree." Since He disagrees, we decide to stay home and read a book, but He says,
"This is still your preference." Gradually, we learn that whenever we have a sense within, the best thing is to kneel down
and pray until we are one with the inward sense. Then, we
are no longer in the state of contradiction. Rather, the more
we pray, the more we sense the presence of God; the more we
pray, the sweeter His presence is. In this way, a part of us
becomes lost and is dissolved in Christ.

No one who is a Christian is exempt from having contradictions. Every Christian goes through a state of contradiction

during the initial phase of his salvation, and the degree of contradiction may become very intense until he reaches a certain level of maturity when the Lord and he have become one. At that stage, the degree of contradiction diminishes because he has matured to a point where he is totally lost in Christ. One who has not reached this state is still spiritually immature.

After we are saved, we usually experience certain contradictions because Christ in us wants us to gain Him, and He also wants to gain us. His intention is to have us mingled with Him. However, because we do not know His intention and are not accustomed to it, the more we pursue Him, the more contradictions we experience. It is as though there is a person within us who is constantly against us. It is as though He disapproves of everything we do in our daily life. It seems in particular that if we do not have a good prayer time in the morning to seek after Him, we do not sense many contradictions throughout the day. But when our prayer times are very good and our fellowship with the Lord increases, the contradictions during the day increase. If we do not pray or have fellowship with the Lord for a month, our living will be carefree and sloppy. However, if we have good prayer times and have good fellowship with the Lord, our contradictions will definitely increase. I believe that we all have this kind of experience. Today if we have a sweet time with the Lord in intimate fellowship and thorough prayer, then amazingly we sense that everything we try to do is not right. Sometimes the bothering gets to a point where we even doubt and ask, "Is it better to pray or not to pray? Why is it that if I do not pray, I am calm and clear, but if I pray, I become confused?" These confusions are all manifestations of the contradictions in us. We are confused because there is an internal conflict. Therefore, the more confusion and contradictions we experience, the better it is. What we should be afraid of is that we have neither confusion nor contradictions. All confused ones are ones with contradictions, and the ones with contradictions are those who have Christ in them as their Lord.

BEING CONFUSED
RATHER THAN BEING COMPLICATED

We are not afraid if someone is confused; rather, we are afraid if someone is not simple. One day there was a brother who was faced with a great difficulty, so he went to see two elderly brothers. After receiving instructions from them on how to resolve the difficulty, he returned home to act according to their advice. However, as he proceeded, there was a forbidding within. Therefore, he became confused. He said, "The words of the two elderly brothers are very clear, but why is it that within me there is a forbidding, a contradiction? What is wrong?" When the event unfolded after a few days, the confused brother realized that what he had sensed as a forbidding was actually the prohibition from the Spirit of the Lord. If he had done according to what the two elderly brothers had advised, the outcome would have been totally different. The two brothers considered the matter according to common experience, and although their consideration was right, the Holy Spirit intervened. We have to understand that this is also a case of contradiction. When a person has contradictions within, this is proof that he is a true Christian. This is why we say that the more contradictions we experience, the better Christians we become. If we do not have contradictions, then there must be problems with us.

If our condition is proper before the Lord, we will have a great deal of contradictions. However, if we have a problem before the Lord and our fellowship with Him has been interrupted, the contradictions will disappear. The sisters experience a great number of contradictions in the matter of attire. Normally, a Christian should have some feelings of contradiction concerning what they wear. If a person claims to be saved and yet has never experienced any contradiction in the matter of clothing himself, then either he is not saved or his salvation is still questionable. A normal Christian most definitely has a great deal of feelings of contradiction. This is because a person who has received the Lord has been lost in Him and has become one with Him. Nevertheless, because we are not easily subdued by the Lord so as to surrender before Him, we always have disputes with Him. We have one idea while the Lord has another idea; we have a desire while the Lord has another desire. Consequently, the two ideas and the two desires bring in contradictions. This is why we say that a Christian who is contradictory within is a true Christian.

ARRIVING AT AN ABSOLUTE ONENESS WITH THE LORD IN THE MIDST OF CONTRADICTIONS

Christians are peculiar and contradictory. Any Christian who has not lived a life of contradictions is not a genuine Christian. A life of contradictions is a life in which we speak a sentence outwardly and there is a disapproval inwardly, or we put on a certain item of clothing outwardly and there is an objection inwardly. This disapproval or objection within comes from Christ Himself. Perhaps we have stayed away from sin, yet we have not committed ourselves to Him to be mingled with Him and be lost in Him. Thus, many things in our Christian life cannot gain His approval. Therefore, as Christians, we go through a series of contradictions from morning to evening. Someone once said, "The more I pray to God, the more confused I get. The more I have fellowship with the Lord, the more I sense that everything is wrong. When I put on shoes, they are not the right shoes. When I put on clothes, they are not the right clothes. It seems that nothing is right." This is wonderful! We have to remember that the more a saved person pursues the Lord, the more he goes through these kinds of contradictions.

Being contradictory is the first stage of the Christian life. In this stage, our thoughts are not the thoughts of the Lord, our will is not His will, our decisions are not His decisions, and our preferences are not His preferences. Therefore, many struggles occur. However, after going through many struggles, one day we will realize that we have decreased while the Lord has increased, that we have lost more ground while the Lord has gained more ground in us, and that we have become less and less while the Lord has become more and more manifest through us. Then we will be completely lost in Him; He and we will be absolutely one. Our will is surrendered to Him; we become Him and He becomes us. Our inclination is His inclination; our preferences are His preferences. In other words, at that time our move is His move. We have become Him. This means that we have attained to the level of spiritual maturity.

Before reaching that stage, however, we have to remember that a Christian is definitely filled with contradictions. It is good to have the contradictions diminished in the course of our pursuit of the Lord, but it is not good to have the contradictions diminished because we have given up on our pursuit of the Lord. If the contradictions decrease because of our obedience, this kind of decrease is good, proper, and necessary. Therefore, we should not be afraid of our inner contradictions. We should not question why we are having so many contradictions when we have already been saved. Do not fear contradictions. The initial stage in the life of a normal Christian is filled with contradictions. The more contradictions he has, the better it is. What we should be afraid of is the lack of the sense of contradiction among us.

CHAPTER SEVEN

TAKING OUR INNERMOST PART
AS THE STARTING POINT

TWO ASPECTS OF A CHRISTIAN

Peculiar before Men

When a Christian lives a normal life before God, he will display certain characteristics that will distinguish him from other people. Titus 2:14 says that God redeemed us from all lawlessness and purified to Himself a particular, or peculiar, people. This means that if a person who has received God's salvation lives in such a salvation to be a normal Christian, his living will appear peculiar to others. Since he does not follow the current of the world as others do, he is peculiar before men. This is a characteristic of a Christian. Christians are different from the worldly people. Those who are in religion are nearly the same as the worldly people, but Christians are not. As those who have received God's salvation, Christians in their normal living are considered peculiar by the world. Therefore, Christians are a peculiar people. This is their manifestation before men.

Contradictory within Himself

On the other hand, a Christian is contradictory within himself. If a Christian lives before God, not departing from the right track, he is seen as peculiar before men. Yet he is also contradictory within himself. The more a person loves the Lord, the more he looks peculiar before men and experiences contradictions within himself. This means that something inside of him disapproves of whatever he does, speaks, and expresses on the outside. His inward being is in opposition, in conflict, and in contradiction with his outward being. Whenever a Christian is neither peculiar without nor contradictory within, then something is wrong with him. Since everything we are speaking here is all within the sphere of Christian living, I would like to present these two aspects as two principles which are before all of us, hoping that we would take hold of them and always use them to measure ourselves. Whenever we lose our outward characteristic of being peculiar and our inward characteristic of being contradictory, we can be sure that we have become degraded. If a Christian is normal before God, he is definitely peculiar before men and contradictory within himself. Being peculiar and being contradictory are the two prerequisites of a person who loves the Lord.

CHRISTIANS CONDUCTING THEMSELVES
WITH THEIR INNERMOST PART
AS THE STARTING POINT

In addition, we have to look at another principle. What should be the starting point of the Christian walk before God? In other words, when a Christian does a certain thing, from where does it originate? For example, someone may ask me—a Christian—to do a certain thing for him. Naturally, I would consider whether this thing is beneficial to him. If it is beneficial, I will do it. This is doing things out of my thinking. If I think it is all right, I will do it; otherwise, I will not do it. I do this thing with my thinking and my insight as the starting point. Another example is when a non-Christian receives an invitation to a banquet, and he begins to consider whether he should go. Of course, such consideration or thinking becomes the starting point of his decision. Normal Christians, however, should conduct themselves not according to their own thinking or insight but according to the sense in their innermost part.

Following the Sense
in Our Innermost Part—the Spirit

Why should our innermost part be the starting point of our Christian walk? We have to realize that our consideration and our discernment are not trustworthy. Even if they are correct, they may still not be pleasing to God, because the starting point is wrong. As Christians, we have the Spirit of God dwelling in us (Rom. 8:11), and we also have God in us (Phil. 2:13; Heb. 13:20-21). This God who is in us lives in our innermost part, which is our spirit. We cannot easily analyze the spirit, but we can sense it. Our innermost feeling is the sense in our spirit. Christ lives in our innermost part, that is, in our spirit (Rom. 8:10; 2 Cor. 13:3, 5). Therefore, to be a normal Christian is to be a Christian according to the sense in our spirit. If we want to be those who follow Christ, we have to follow the sense in our innermost part because that is where Christ dwells.

I hope that we would not treat this matter lightly. In particular, the newly saved ones should pay much attention to it. Many Christians have a great lack in their spiritual experience because they do not understand this matter. Religions always focus on teaching people outwardly; their starting point is from without. But God's salvation is not like that. After we have received God's salvation, this salvation abides in us and requires us to have our starting point from within. From that time onward, we should no longer walk merely according to our own discernment and perception. Rather, we must walk according to the sense in our deepest part, that is, the sense in our spirit, because Christ lives in our spirit, our innermost part.

Let me illustrate. Suppose one day as we are praying and pursuing the Lord, we sense in our innermost part that we should no longer wear the clothing that we are wearing. It is not a matter of whether we like or dislike this clothing; rather, it is a matter of having a sense of disapproval while we are praying. We feel uncomfortable if we continue to wear this clothing. Perhaps we would seek out fellowship and ask a certain brother regarding this matter. Perhaps that brother would gently say, "This clothing looks fine. I do not know why you should not wear it," yet we still feel uncomfortable despite what he says. What should we do then? Should we follow his outward advice or should we act according to our inward sense? Regardless of anything else, a normal Christian must take his inner sense as the starting point of his daily walk.

Not Reasoning

Many newly saved ones, due to the freshness of life, are quite accurate in their consciousness about sin. On the contrary, many who have been Christians for years are mixed up and frequently lead others down the wrong path. We all know that the skin of the soles of our feet is hardened and thickened through much walking and consequently becomes insensitive. The skin of infants is soft and thus very sensitive. There are some who love the Lord and are constantly dealt with by Him. Such ones do not have a "hardened, thickened skin." On the contrary, they have become "rejuvenated" within. This means that they have become experienced. Having been dealt with and broken before God, they have become soft. We may meet such a one and ask him, "Yesterday morning after praying, I did not have the peace to wear this clothing. What shall I do?" Because he is an experienced person before the Lord, instead of lying to you, he will say, "Since you do not have the peace, then you should not wear it." He will not reason or argue.

However, some will reason or argue on behalf of others. Some long-time Christians apparently have no big mistakes in their life, but because their fellowship with the Lord has been broken, they do not care about God at all. If such a Christian would hear our question, he would say, "What is wrong with this? This clothing is quite elegant. Why should you feel uncomfortable wearing it?" Although he is saved, there is a problem with his fellowship with the Lord. If we act according to his words, we will be led astray. If we wear that clothing, no one would criticize us and say that we are wrong, nor would anyone condemn us according to the teachings of the entire Bible. Nevertheless, we have made a mistake, not in violation of a regulation but in violation of a basic principle. Why is this? This is because we Christians must take our inner sense as the starting point. Strictly speaking, everything we do must originate from our innermost part. For example, Brother Hwang asked me if it is all right to enter into a business partnership with another brother. If I am experienced before God and if I fear Him, I will not make a decision for him. Rather, I will remind him and say, "Have you gone before God to pray about this matter? Have you sought for an answer before Him? Have you fellowshipped with Him? Do you have any sense in your innermost part?"

A certain brother came and talked to me about his marriage, asking, "What is the proper way to have a Christian wedding?" I said, "Whenever I watch a wedding being held in the assembly hall of the church in Taipei, it is as if I am looking at a condition of leprosy. Some unclean things which are condemned before God are manifested there. The whole situation makes me feel very uncomfortable. The guests all desire to bless the new couple, but the way the bride walks down the aisle and the way she adorns herself have completely canceled out God's blessing and God's presence." Nothing is more sensitive than the sense in our spirit. If a person does not have a cold, his sense of smell is very keen. He can smell the aroma of any fragrant thing around him. Likewise, he can smell the stench of any odorous thing nearby. The sense of the human spirit, however, is the most sensitive of all. Even our insight is not as keen as our spirit. The most sensitive part in us is our human spirit. It is not necessary to tell others whether we have prayed or not. They know our situation immediately after they come into contact with us. Therefore, I said to that brother, "I have offended all those who were married in the Taipei meeting hall by saying that nearly all the weddings held there were expressions of leprosy. But I believe that the God whom I serve condemns likewise."

Concerning our past practices, I do not dare to say anything good or bad in order to influence others, but I dare say that there is neither God's blessing nor God's presence. I told that brother, "Concerning your wedding, I cannot tell you what to do, but you know what you should do. If a person has been suffering from a temperature of 104 degrees Fahrenheit, is there any use to tell him not to also have a temperature of 104 degrees about his wedding? Whatever you say will be futile. If someone wants to be leprous, let him be, because no one will be able to hold him back." Then the brother said,

"That is wrong." However, this is not merely an issue of right or wrong; rather, it is a situation which is outside God and in which there is no contact with God. As a rule, a good wedding meeting is a meeting in which we have a feast together with the Lord. A wedding in God is a wedding with His special presence. The wedding meetings in the past, however, were devoid of the Lord's presence. Finally, I told the brother that the two persons who are to be married must go before God to pray and then do according to what they sense in their prayer. In any case, they should do everything according to the sense of peace in their innermost part.

Bringing All Things before the Lord

As a rule, a Christian must use his inner sense as the starting point. Basically, he does not need to seek out everyone for advice. Perhaps some weddings are from Babylon, while others may even be from the bottomless pit; not all weddings originate from Jerusalem. Since we are saved, we need to bring every matter before the Lord and pray, "Lord, since You live in me, what would You like to do?" This is being a Christian. I believe that hardly anyone has prayed to the Lord about every matter relating to his wedding. Many Christians who are getting married focus on the outward considerations rather than the inward peace as their starting point. As a result, a few weeks after their wedding, they have to go before God and ask for forgiveness. The fact that they have to ask for forgiveness is a strong indication that they did not do things according to the inner sense. Do not do things according to outward considerations, outward customs, human regulations, human opinions, and human endorsements, all of which are condemned before God. We have to learn to conduct ourselves according to our innermost part.

If a young man comes to ask us, "I am going to be engaged, so what should I do now? And what shall I do when I get married later?" Now, of course, we know how to respond and say, "I cannot decide for you. I cannot be your lord or master." In fact, though, when some older ones hear about two young people getting married, they would eagerly offer their advice even before being asked. These ones do not understand what it means to be a Christian. Once there was a brother who came to me to talk about his marriage, and he gave me all the details of his situation. I simply told him, "Brother, have you seriously prayed about this matter before God? Have you turned this matter over to God? Are you in the hands of God? What is the sense in your innermost part?" He said, "I have prayed for this matter for a long time. But the more I prayed, the more confused I have become. Therefore, I would like to hear what you have to say because you have a deeper experience in the Lord. If you say it is all right, then it must be all right. If you say it is not all right, then it must not be all right." When I heard this, I thought, this is serious! Therefore, I dared not say whether or not it was all right. I simply told him, "I cannot decide for you. You have to bring this matter before the Lord." That brother expected me to come up with a plan or make a decision for him, but I could not. Finally, I told him, "Do not be distressed over this. This matter is quite simple. You need to put it before God, commit yourself to Him, and ask Him for guidance. You can tell Him, 'If this matter is of You, cause me to become so clear about it within. If this is not of You, then let me sense the blockage.'" It is so simple. We all have to learn to bring all our matters before God and to live in our innermost part.

Doing All Things from Within

In order to be a normal Christian before God we need to learn to do everything from within, from our innermost part. When we help others, we should learn to turn them inward, into the innermost part of their being. Do not draw up a set of human regulations for them, do not ask them to do things according to our insight, and do not make decisions for them. These things are unbecoming to Christians and are beyond the bounds of the Christian living. Many elderly Christians have not been dealt with in their flesh or broken in their disposition. Such ones are full of opinions, methods, and ideas whenever people ask them for advice. This is not being a Christian but rather being a Mr. Know-it-all.

Christians live before God and learn to bring other people's affairs as well as their own before the Lord. They do not dare to make decisions for themselves. Instead, they wait for God's clear leading within them. This is being a Christian. We should be Christians not outwardly but inwardly. To be a Christian outwardly is to be a Christian apart from Christ. Human views, human methods, Christian traditions, and even biblical teachings are all outward if they have not passed through the inner sense. Being an outward Christian is quite superficial and is of no value before God. A genuine Christian does everything from within. He brings all matters to prayer and waits for an inner sense before making a decision. Even a new believer should know and behave in this manner. This type of person surely has the inner peace, rest, strength, and vigor.

Real Christians do not care for outward rituals; rather, they care for the inner life and spirit (Rom. 2:29) What may be proper and good outwardly may not necessarily be proper and good before God. What counts before God is to be proper and good inwardly. Until now many Christians have not yet been walking on this path. Although many people have embraced Christianity, only a few have truly lived this way before God. Some have been saved and have received blessings from God, but they live neither in their spirit nor in God's blessings. They still do things according to traditions and customs and according to what others say or observe. In other words, they act according to outward factors. We have to learn to be simple, knowing nothing about natural affections and Christian traditions but knowing only that Christ lives in us and that we can have fellowship with Him. We go ahead and do a certain thing whenever Christ in us gives us the peace. We stop whenever the inner peace is absent. We will not care for what other people say. We care only for what Christ says in us and the inner sense He gives us.

In conclusion, Christians are peculiar before men, contradictory within themselves, and live in their deepest part before God. Some Christians encountered many difficulties and made many mistakes when they first began to walk on this path. Although they have made mistakes outwardly while living before God, in principle they are still right. Therefore, Christians should live and walk in a hidden way;

they should not make a public show. Although Christians should not do things stealthily, they should not make a public display either. Some people like to make a show when they perform a good deed. This is not the Christian life. Genuine Christians live before God. Regardless of how many good deeds they perform, no one knows except their Lord and themselves. This is the principle in Matthew chapter six. Sometimes a person prays a little bit and eagerly desires to be heard by others or be followed by others with more prayers. However, those who are with him will not sense that his prayer carries any weight. The normal situation is that although you are humble, you do not display your humility before men; although you are meek, you do not show off your meekness before men. There are times when people who are being humble or meek cause us to be uncomfortable and uneasy. This is because they are doing it not from within but from without.

A SPIRITUAL MAN
BEING SPONTANEOUS AND INGENUOUS

Forgive me for saying that many Christians like to imitate others. In particular, they like to imitate the seminary students in their way of walking while holding the Bible and gazing heavenward every few steps. That is to be pretentious. Please keep in mind that the more spiritual a person is, the more spontaneous, ingenuous, and ordinary he is. When you consider his humility, he does not look like one who is humble. When you consider his meekness, he does not look like one who is meek. You cannot see meekness in him just as you cannot see rudeness. He is so spontaneous and ingenuous, without any affectation.

In the Middle Ages in France, there was a renowned preacher who was well praised and whose preaching was very well received. Once he visited a place and many came to welcome him, but he eluded them. Instead, he went to a playground to be with a group of children. He found a wooden board and placed two children on one end, himself on the other end, and began to play seesaw with them. Those who were welcoming him searched all over only to find him playing seesaw with some children. Thus, many of them felt like cold water had been poured on them. They could not understand how a spiritual man could play with children. Consequently, some began to say that he was not spiritual. Later in his own words, he said that he would rather be considered not spiritual than spiritual.

OUR SPIRITUALITY BEING A MATTER BEFORE GOD

Whether or not we are spiritual is a matter before God, not men. We are not Christians if we are Christians merely outwardly. We are Christians only if we are Christians inwardly. The Lord Jesus said that we should not let the left hand know what the right hand is doing (Matt. 6:3). A weighty Christian is a Christian inwardly; he is an inward Christian. Such a Christian is peculiar before men and contradictory within himself. Moreover, he does all things before God with his deepest part as the starting point. Therefore, Paul said, "The spiritual man discerns all things, but he himself is discerned by no one" (1 Cor. 2:15). Why is it that no one can discern a spiritual man? It is because outwardly a spiritual man is very plain and, like Paul, may even be weak in bodily presence and contemptible in speech (2 Cor. 10:10). Yet he has the spiritual weightiness within, and he is a person who conducts himself in Christ and who lives before God. This is a Christian.

CHAPTER EIGHT

THE LEADING IN A CHRISTIAN

A Christian possesses at least four things. First, he has Christ; a person is not a Christian if he does not have Christ. Second, he has the Bible; third, he has the church; and fourth, he has fellow Christians or companions in the Lord. In addition, such a Christian has four characteristics.

CHARACTERISTICS OF A CHRISTIAN
Peculiar before Men

First, a Christian is peculiar in the eyes of the world. He is distinctly different from the worldly people. If a Christian walks like the worldly people, even though he may not be a false Christian, he is surely a questionable Christian. A normal Christian is most certainly peculiar before men.

Full of Contradictions within Himself

Second, if a Christian lives before God and maintains fellowship with Him, his inward sense and outward behavior usually are in contradiction. His inner being often disapproves of his outward living, attitudes, and speaking. In other words, a proper Christian always experiences contradictions between his inward sense and his outward behavior. This is normal. Therefore, a Christian is both peculiar and full of contradictions.

Taking the Innermost Part as the Starting Point before God

Third, if a Christian lives before God, he will do all things from within his innermost part. He is reluctant to show off his good deeds because he does everything inwardly. A Christian who acts and moves from within is spontaneous, ingenuous, and honest, without outward pretense and imitation. Whatever he does in his daily walk, he does it out of his innermost part, because that is where the Spirit of God dwells. He takes his innermost part as the starting point of his walk; this means that God is his starting point. Therefore, a Christian lives, walks, and has his being not from without but from deep within. Inwardly he is in the light and he is good, while outwardly he is spontaneous and does not engage in mere outward activities.

In summary, the first three characteristics of a Christian include his being peculiar before men, his being contradictory within himself, and his walking before God with his innermost part as the starting point. People in the world all plunge into the current of this age, but a genuine Christian does not follow the current, is not fashioned according to this age (Rom. 12:2), and most certainly does not follow the bad examples of others. Hence, he is seen as peculiar. Inwardly he has the presence of God, the consciousness of Christ, and the enlightening of the Holy Spirit, which all constantly disapprove of his outward walk and living. Others may not condemn him and may instead even praise him. Inwardly, however, he always condemns himself for not coming up to God's standard. This comes from his having fellowship with the Lord. The more he fellowships with the Lord and draws near to Him, the more contradictions he experiences. The more he enjoys the presence of the Lord, the more he feels that many aspects of his outward living are incompatible with God's will and God's holiness. Therefore, his inward being always disagrees with his outward conduct, and he constantly has a sense of contradiction between the inward and the outward. Moreover, a proper Christian is one who does all things before God out of his innermost part.

Being Led in All Things

Besides being peculiar, being contradictory, and taking his innermost part as the starting point, a Christian is led by the Lord in all things. What is a leading? Perhaps this word is difficult to understand. In fact, the Word of God speaks a great deal about the matter of leading. Most people, however, do not speak much about it. What does it mean to be led? For example, I may want to go to a certain place but do not know the direction, so I get someone to lead me there—he walks before me while I follow from behind. This applies not only to walking but also to the handling of affairs. This is what the Bible refers to as leading.

A saved one must be led by God in all things, such as how he should behave, how he should walk, and how he should live. Generally speaking, he must be led by God in all things, great or small, that are related to his food, clothing, shelter, and transportation, as well as in the things related to his family, to himself, and to his education or knowledge. No matter how people praise us, if there are still some areas in our life and within us that are not under the leading of God, we know that there are still problems in us.

A normal Christian is one who is led even in the smallest matter of his living. Someone may ask, "To what degree of smallness is the smallest matter?" According to what I have learned, we have to fellowship with God and be led even concerning the style of our haircut. We also need to be led in the matter of determining how much to spend for a pair of shoes. Ordinarily, most Christians are so competent that they do not care about the Lord's will and good pleasure. It is not until great things occur that they would pray, "Lord, I am about to be married. What should I do? I have to search for a job. How should I proceed with it?" In other words, they pray and inquire about important matters but not about the trivial things in their daily living. This type of Christian is abnormal and unhealthy. A normal and healthy Christian is one who lives with the Lord and who brings everything, both great and small, before Him.

BEING LED TO BE CONSTITUTED
WITH THE NATURE OF GOD

In reality, what we consider great things are small things before God. What kind of great things do we have? Our stature is about six feet at most. The great things in our lives are small things in God's eyes. Nevertheless, God desires that we inquire of Him even in the smallest things. For example, humanly speaking, we do not like for our children to do things without our knowledge. Even in trivial things such as eating an apple or a piece of cracker, we like for them to tell us. Parents are not happy if their child is so capable in doing everything that he does not need them all day long. Bosses dislike to be troubled by their employees; parents, however, are not bothered by children continually coming to them. When one child comes to let his parents know that he wants an apple and another child comes to tell them that he wants to play ball, how satisfied the parents are! Therefore, a Christian should not just pray every day. Rather, he should pray and fellowship with the Lord every moment of the day. For example, before you set out to go to Kaoshiung, you have to ask God, "O God, I want to go to Kaoshiung; what do You think about this?" After you have prayed and have sensed the peace to go, you should inquire again as to which day you should go. Once you are clear about the day, you should inquire further, "Lord, which scheduled train should I take?" God is not afraid to be bothered by us, so we should feel free to seek Him. In this way, not only are we blessed in the matter for which we inquire, but through our seeking we also have more fellowship with God and, consequently, we are filled with God's nature.

I used to go to Peiping (Beijing), where there was a brother who was born in a certain place in South America that had been under the rule of the British people. Outwardly that brother looked just like us, having the same skin color and eye color as we have, but his temperament was the temperament of an Englishman, and he also spoke like an Englishman. He was a very good friend of mine, so I used to stay with him whenever I visited Peiping. Once I told him, "You are evidently a Chinese, but your temperament is totally the temperament of a foreigner." Why is it that he as a Chinese behaved like an Englishman? It is because from the day he was born, his daily contacts were with Englishmen. Therefore, he had been infused with the British nature and temperament. This shows us why Christians must always pray. Through our constant inquiring before God, we are being constituted with His nature and elements.

After we are saved in the Lord, God desires that we would be filled by Him and be like Him, so that His nature, life, and elements will be constituted into us. One thing is certain and clear: If a person decides every matter according to his own discernment, handles every matter according to his own methods, and makes every choice according to his own preference, then when people touch him, they can only sense that he is a capable person, a person with great decisiveness. They cannot sense the flavor and presence of God in him. Conversely, if a person inquires before God concerning everything, then spontaneously God's view becomes his view, God's nature becomes his nature, and God's elements become his elements. For example, if we see a person regularly and are constantly in contact with him, unconsciously we become somewhat like him. A husband and wife are the best example; after they have been married a long time, they begin increasingly to look alike.

In 1934 a young brother in Tientsin who was learning to serve the Lord was always by my side helping me. One year he went to Shanghai. After he gave the first message, many were astonished at how his intonation and gestures were exactly like mine. When we are with someone every day in an intimate way—we may even be living with him—his disposition and intonation spontaneously become our disposition and intonation. Similarly, if a Christian constantly seeks after God and has fellowship with God, then God's nature will spontaneously become his. If a Christian seeks God only to be prosperous or successful, that is a small matter. But if we believe that the purpose of Christians living on earth is merely for success and blessings, this is to not esteem the salvation of God highly. Christians should not care about having a successful career or a prosperous way. Rather, they should care only about their fellowship with God. If a Christian maintains a fellowship with God that is increasingly intimate and deep, he will be able to bring salvation to others even to the extent that he will become a blessing to people. Wherever he goes, God's salvation also goes there to reach everyone through him. He does not care about the success and fortune of people. He simply cares that the salvation of God has a way to go out through him. Such a Christian is a weighty Christian.

It is not possible, however, to be such a Christian by imitation and affectation. Similarly, there is no way for that Christian brother who was born and raised in South America to act Chinese because he has been with English people from his youth and has gradually been constituted with the nature of an Englishman. If we have fellowship with God daily, the nature and elements of God will spontaneously be constituted into our being. Accordingly, the salvation of God and the blessings of God can be dispensed to others through us. This is why we should draw near to God, pray, and be led by God so that the elements of God can be constituted into us.

BEING LED TO DISCUSS EVERYTHING WITH GOD

About a hundred years ago there was a spiritual man in England named George Müller, who founded an orphanage. He was a German who became a British citizen after he went to England to preach the gospel. His wife also was British. When he was led by God to establish an orphanage, he did not do any fundraising; he only prayed. He was a person who asked God concerning all things. We may say that he was one who sought after God through prayer all day long. On the one hand, he was managing the affairs. On the other hand, he was looking to God, fellowshipping with God, and discussing things with God. If I remember correctly, whenever he met with someone or tried to resolve a difficult issue, he would be talking to men outwardly and speaking to God inwardly, just like the businessmen in Shanghai who always have two phones at the same time, one in each hand. This encourages me very much. Not only did Müller commit matters to prayer, but even in the midst of discussion with others, he also continued to ask God and seek His leading. In his autobiography he said that before he would do anything, he would ask God if a certain matter pleased Him. Then he would ask if God wanted him to do it, because God might want something to be done in the universe but not necessarily through him. When

Müller was clear that God wanted him to do it, the third thing he would do was to ask God when He wanted him to do it. The fourth thing was to ask God where to do it. The fifth thing was to ask God how to do it. Müller would bring these five points before God and would carefully ask, "O God, is it Your intention to do this thing? If you do not intend to do this, then I will not touch it or do it." Müller was one who would bring every matter, whether big or small, to God for consultation. This was his practice moment by moment.

There was a Christian boss who, while transacting business with others, would often say, "I have to go back and consult my Boss." The other party would ask, "Who is your Boss?" He would respond with a grin, "You have your boss, and I have my Boss too. My Boss is One whom you have not known." What he meant was he would carefully consult with the Lord because the Lord was his Boss. A proper Christian is one who learns to live before the Lord daily and who practices to be led by Him. Otherwise, there is definitely something wrong with this Christian, even if people perceive him as right and proper. When we shop for a suit, we have to ask the Lord what color or style to choose. If we think that it is all right to purchase the suit as long as we have enough money in our pocket and the suit fits us just fine, then we have a big problem. People will begin to put question marks on us. They will ask, "Is this Christian inside or outside of God, or perhaps has he not yet entered into the grace of God?"

A proper Christian lives and dwells with the Lord. The Lord is his Master, his Counterpart, and his Companion. Daily he lives before the Lord, walks with the Lord, dwells with the Lord, and rests with the Lord. This is a good and proper Christian. Such a Christian will always be led by the Lord and have the consciousness of the Lord. He knows what the Lord wants him to do, and where and when he should do it. He is enlightened, fresh, pure, and full of the presence of the Lord. He is quick to sense problems that arise because he lives before God. Whenever we meet him, we feel as if we are meeting God. We can always sense that God is upon him and in him. Why? It is because he is a person who fellowships with God and consults with God. He does not have his own natural discernment or his own arrangement. Everything he does comes out of the Lord and is unto the Lord. Whatever he does is under the leading of God.

THE MEANING OF BEING LED

To help us learn the lesson of being led, first we must be clear about the meaning of being led. We usually think that the purpose of being led is to gain some benefit for ourselves. This is an improper concept. The Chinese people pay too much attention to benefits and fortune. Their minds are filled with hopes for longevity, blessings, and peace. Sometimes people ask me, "Sir, if I believe in Jesus, will He be more effective than Buddha? Can He make my son wealthy and my daughter-in-law bear children?" To them, believing in Jesus is the same as worshipping Buddha. Their minds are filled with peace and wealth. Many people believe in the Lord to obtain blessings, peace, and prosperity. The Lord has been kind and considerate towards us and has answered some prayers of this kind. However, the Lord's ultimate goal in answering our prayer is not just that we may obtain peace but that He may gain us and fill us, so that we may have His nature and His image. The Lord is working towards this goal.

HOW TO BE LED

The Bible tells us that the Lord is the Potter, and we are the clay (Rom. 9:21). Oftentimes a potter will pick up some unmolded clay, pat it gently, shave off the excess, and make straight the crooked angles. Eventually a shape is formed, and the clay is burned in fire. Christians are like clay in the hands of the Lord, and He intends to make us into His vessels. Therefore, we have to be led. First, we must not consider blessings our priority. If we do, we cannot be led by the Lord. Someone asked me, "I have some problems. If I pray earnestly, will God turn around the difficulties?" I said, "I do not know the pathway that God has arranged for you. He can turn around the situation, but I do not know if He is willing to do that for you. He wants to place you in a distressing situation so that you may be burned and burned again. Through the burning He can make you into a precious vessel in His hand." We should not use our believing in the Lord as a means to obtain some blessings according to our will and not according to His will.

Second, in order to be led by the Lord we need to conduct ourselves in the world not in fleshly wisdom but in the grace of God (2 Cor. 1:12). A person who depends on his abilities cannot receive leading from the Lord. Everyone who has been led by the Lord has crushed his fleshly wisdom and his abilities. Perhaps we are afraid that if our abilities are demolished, we will not have anything and will not be able to do anything. In reality, though, the most competent person is one whose abilities and fleshly wisdom have been broken. Is God not more capable than we are? Is God not wiser than we are? There was an elderly Christian in London who had a very intelligent son. Every morning, when her son was about to go to his office, she would repeatedly remind her son to not live according to the wisdom of his flesh but according to the grace of God.

Third, we have to learn to consecrate ourselves to God. A person who has not consecrated himself to God cannot be led. We have to absolutely consecrate to God our family and our whole being with all that we have and all that we are. Only then can the Lord lead us. Then we can learn to rely on the Lord and ask for His leading in big things and small things. For example, someone may ask us, "Would you like to come with me to Tamsui for a walk?" We do not have to rigidly kneel down to pray, but we have to inquire of God inwardly, bringing the matter before Him to discuss it with Him. If we would follow the Lord, walk in His path, and commit ourselves to God, discussing all matters, big or small, with Him, and clearly receiving His leading before we take action, then we are truly walking in and with the Lord.

In summary, Christians possess four things—Christ, the Bible, the church, and fellow Christians as their companions. Christians also have four characteristics—being peculiar, being full of contradictions, taking their innermost part as the starting point, and being led. This is wonderful. If, as Christians, we have reached a point where we are simply following the current in society, then we have degraded and have lost our normal Christian status. Conversely, if we live before God and maintain fellowship with Him, we are definitely peculiar before men, we are full of contradictions within ourselves—being always against ourselves, and we conduct ourselves as Christians from within our innermost part. In addition, we do not make decisions for ourselves, nor are we individualistic, but we are daily led by the Lord, allowing Him to make decisions for us and to walk and live with us. We are not careless. Rather, we are living before God, walking with Him, and being led by Him in big things and small things.

ABOUT THE AUTHOR

Witness Lee was born in 1905 in northern China and raised in a Christian family. At age 19 he was fully captured for Christ and immediately consecrated himself to preach the gospel for the rest of his life. Early in his service, he met Watchman Nee, a renowned preacher, teacher, and writer. Witness Lee labored together with Watchman Nee under his direction. In 1934 Watchman Nee entrusted Witness Lee with the responsibility for his publication operation, called the Shanghai Gospel Bookroom.

Prior to the Communist takeover in 1949, Witness Lee was sent by Watchman Nee and his other co-workers to Taiwan to insure that the things delivered to them by the Lord would not be lost. Watchman Nee instructed Witness Lee to continue the former's publishing operation abroad as the Taiwan Gospel Bookroom, which has been publicly recognized as the publisher of Watchman Nee's works outside China. Witness Lee's work in Taiwan manifested the Lord's abundant blessing. From a mere 350 believers, newly fled from the mainland, the churches in Taiwan grew to 20,000 in five years.

In 1962 Witness Lee felt led of the Lord to come to the United States, settling in California. During his 35 years of service in the U.S., he ministered in weekly meetings and weekend conferences, delivering several thousand spoken messages. Much of his speaking has since been published as over 400 titles. Many of these have been translated into over fourteen languages. He gave his last public conference in February 1997 at the age of 91.

He leaves behind a prolific presentation of the truth in the Bible. His major work, *Life-study of the Bible,* comprises over 25,000 pages of commentary on every book of the Bible from the perspective of the believers' enjoyment and experience of God's divine life in Christ through the Holy Spirit. Witness Lee was the chief editor of a new translation of the New Testament into Chinese called the Recovery Version and directed the translation of the same into English. The Recovery Version also appears in a number of other languages. He provided an extensive body of footnotes, outlines, and spiritual cross references. A radio broadcast of his messages can be heard on Christian radio stations in the United States. In 1965 Witness Lee founded Living Stream Ministry, a non-profit corporation, located in Anaheim, California, which officially presents his and Watchman Nee's ministry.

Witness Lee's ministry emphasizes the experience of Christ as life and the practical oneness of the believers as the Body of Christ. Stressing the importance of attending to both these matters, he led the churches under his care to grow in Christian life and function. He was unbending in his conviction that God's goal is not narrow sectarianism but the Body of Christ. In time, believers began to meet simply as the church in their localities in response to this conviction. In recent years a number of new churches have been raised up in Russia and in many eastern European countries.

OTHER BOOKS PUBLISHED BY
Living Stream Ministry

Titles by Witness Lee:

Abraham—Called by God	0-7363-0359-6
The Experience of Life	0-87083-417-7
The Knowledge of Life	0-87083-419-3
The Tree of Life	0-87083-300-6
The Economy of God	0-87083-415-0
The Divine Economy	0-87083-268-9
God's New Testament Economy	0-87083-199-2
The World Situation and God's Move	0-87083-092-9
Christ vs. Religion	0-87083-010-4
The All-inclusive Christ	0-87083-020-1
Gospel Outlines	0-87083-039-2
Character	0-87083-322-7
The Secret of Experiencing Christ	0-87083-227-1
The Life and Way for the Practice of the Church Life	0-87083-785-0
The Basic Revelation in the Holy Scriptures	0-87083-105-4
The Crucial Revelation of Life in the Scriptures	0-87083-372-3
The Spirit with Our Spirit	0-87083-798-2
Christ as the Reality	0-87083-047-3
The Central Line of the Divine Revelation	0-87083-960-8
The Full Knowledge of the Word of God	0-87083-289-1
Watchman Nee—A Seer of the Divine Revelation ...	0-87083-625-0

Titles by Watchman Nee:

How to Study the Bible	0-7363-0407-X
God's Overcomers	0-7363-0433-9
The New Covenant	0-7363-0088-0
The Spiritual Man 3 volumes	0-7363-0269-7
Authority and Submission	0-7363-0185-2
The Overcoming Life	1-57593-817-0
The Glorious Church	0-87083-745-1
The Prayer Ministry of the Church	0-87083-860-1
The Breaking of the Outer Man and the Release ...	1-57593-955-X
The Mystery of Christ	1-57593-954-1
The God of Abraham, Isaac, and Jacob	0-87083-932-2
The Song of Songs	0-87083-872-5
The Gospel of God 2 volumes	1-57593-953-3
The Normal Christian Church Life	0-87083-027-9
The Character of the Lord's Worker	1-57593-322-5
The Normal Christian Faith	0-87083-748-6
Watchman Nee's Testimony	0-87083-051-1

Available at
Christian bookstores, or contact Living Stream Ministry
2431 W. La Palma Ave. • Anaheim, CA 92801
1-800-549-5164 • www.livingstream.com